Bulbs
for All Seasons

Pierre Gingras

FIREFLY BOOKS

A FIREFLY BOOK

Published by Firefly Books Ltd., 2001

First English language edition © Firefly Books Ltd. 2001

First published in French by Les Éditions de l'Homme, 1999, a division of the Sogides Group

First Printing
National Library of Canada Cataloguing in Publication Data
Gingras, Pierre,
 Bulbs for all seasons

Translation of: Des bulbes en toutes saisons.
Includes bibliographical references and index.
ISBN 1-55209-587-8

1. Bulbs.   2. Bulbs – Quebec (Province).   3. Floriculture.
4. Flower gardening.   I. Ballantyne, Michael.   II. Title.

SB425.G5613   2001   635.9'1532   C2001-930405-6

U. S. Cataloging-in-Publication Data
(Library of Congress Standards)

Gingras, Pierre.
 Bulbs for all seasons/Pierre Gingras. – 1st U.S. ed.
[288] p.; col. ill.: cm.
Originally published: "Des bulbes en toutes saisons";
Les Éditions de l'Homme, 2000.
Includes bibliographical references and index.
Summary: Illustrated reference to bulbs and gardening with bulbs.
ISBN 1-55209-587-8 (pbk)
1. Bulbs.   2. Gardening.   I. Title.
635.9/4   21   2001   CIP

Published in Canada in 2001 by
Firefly Books Ltd.
3680 Victoria Park Avenue
Willowdale, Ontario M2H 3K1

Published in the United States in 2001 by
Firefly Books (U.S.) Inc.
P.O. Box 1338, Ellicott Station
Buffalo, New York 14205

Printed in Canada

Translated by Michael Ballantyne

On cover:
Bégonia Pacific Hybrid®, 'Peach & Bronze Picotee',
 Simple Pleasures
Crocus 'Ruby Giant', Internationaal Bloembollen Centrum,
 Hillegom-Holland
Tulipe 'Beauty of Apeldoorn', Internationaal Bloembollen
 Centrum
Dahlia semi-cactus 'Jeanne d'Arc', Internationaal Bloembollen
 Centrum

Page 283: Facing page: A garden of lilies. Jacques Allard
Page 284: "Star Gazer" Oriental lily, one of the most popular
varieties. Internationaal Bloembollen Centrum
Page 285: "Pinelands Pam" fimbriated, or fringed, dahlia.
Michèle Cartier

Contents

Spring 37

Indigenous Plants 128

Summer

For my granddaughter, Emma,
a spring flower in her own right

$\mathcal{A}$CKNOWLEDGEMENTS

This book would never have been published without the efforts of many collaborators. My thanks first of all to *La Presse*, where I work, whose editors gave me the necessary time off — with pay. Thanks also to the readers of my column, whose encouragement and suggestions have helped me enormously over the years.

I am also indebted to Internationaal Bloembollen Centrum, in Holland, and its Canadian representative, Carol Cowan of the Information Center for Flowering Bulbs in Toronto, for information and photographic material.

Among those who have supplied much appreciated assistance are: Paul Jansen, Quebec representative for Vanhof and Blokker, bulb wholesalers; Michel-André Otis, horticulturalist at the Montreal Botanical Gardens, who reviewed the manuscript; Guy Viandier, who oversees Norseco's experimental gardens at Boisbriand; Nicole Bolduc, of the Friends of the Van den Hende Garden in Sainte-Foy; Patricia Gallant, horticultural expert at the Métis Gardens; Raymond Perreault, of Serres Perreault in Warwick; Melinda Wilson, lily grower in Racine, Quebec; Monique Dumas-Quesnel, bulb buyer for Horticlub, Norseco in Laval; Réjean Geoffrion and André Jasmin, of Pépinière Jasmin in Montreal.

Special thanks to the generous people who offered photographs: the staff photographers at *La Presse*, in particular Pierre McCann; Michèle Cartier, president of the Quebec Dahlia Society; Jacques Allard, secretary of the Friends of the Van den Hende Garden; Cruickshank's, B.C.; Vanhof and Blokker; and the Montreal Botanical Gardens.

Rémi Lemée, *La Presse*

Eremurus himalaicus *and Oriental poppies growing in the author's garden.*

11

$\mathscr{P}$REFACE

$\mathscr{I}$ still remember the winter, some years ago, when I "forced" about 1000 bulbs in my basement. What madness! you'll say. At least that's what my better half thought when she went down one day to help me with the watering. But the results were extraordinary. At least 24 varieties of tulip, four crocus cultivars, as well as daffodils, anemones and ranunculus. A veritable indoor garden.

That was the winter I fell in love with Marjolettii, a delicate tulip with tiny blooms, and its distinguished cousin "Fusilier," which produces several flowers on each stem.

The fever has abated a little since then but I'm still just as passionate about bulbs. Spring, summer, fall or winter, there's always a bulbous plant flowering at my place — in the garden or in the house.

This book has one objective, and only one: to share my passion for these plants, many of which are relatively unknown.

The varieties presented in the following pages are nearly all available at local nurseries or from catalogues. Moreover, their availability has to a large extent dictated the choice of varieties and cultivars described here. I have certainly had to limit the selection, which explains why some varieties — especially those considered as perennials, such as *liatris* and lily of the valley — are not included.

As you leaf through these pages, let yourself be enchanted by the beauty and the individuality of plants that for the most part need only minimum care. And when the time comes to watch the spectacular flowering of an *Eremurus,* or Star-of-Bethlehem, to savour the scent of a Gladiolus callianthus or to decorate your table with a bright red Crocosmia, you'll never look at your own garden in quite the same way again.

Fritillaria imperialis *"Lutea"*.

WHAT IS A BULB?

Bulbous plants make up a little botanical universe of their own. They all consist of an organ, whether it be a bulb, a corm, a rhizome, or a tuber, in which reserves of energy are accumulated, allowing it to produce flowers at the appropriate time.

From a physiological and anatomical point of view, there are important differences between the tunic-clad tulip bulb, the lily's tunicless bulb, the corm of the gladiolus, the tuberous root of the dahlia, and the rhizome of the trillium.

1	OXALIS ADENOPHYLLA	7	NARCISSUS	11	ALLIUM MOLY
2	TULIPA	8	HYACINTHUS	12	CHIONODOXA
3	NARCISSUS	9	CROCUS	13	ANEMONE
4	EREMURUS	10	MUSCARI	14	HYACINTHUS
5	ALLIUM GIGANTEUM				
6	FRITILLARIA IMPERALIS				

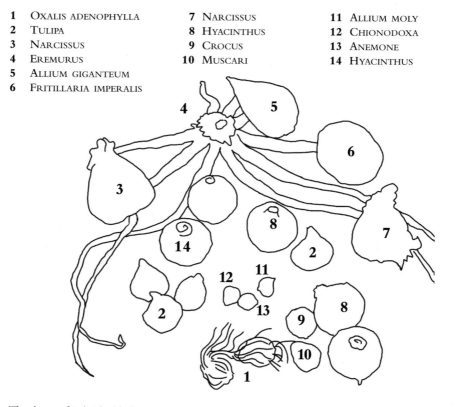

The shapes of individual bulbs vary considerably. Eremurus *and* oxalis *are especially distinctive.*

The real bulb

The amaryllis, the tulip and the lily all represent the tried-and-true bulb. The true bulb is formed by a floral bud and enclosed in successive layers of fleshy scales that function as a storage reserve. The bottom part of the bulb is composed of a basal plate from which the roots emerge. The stalk rises from the center of the bulb.

The large layers of the amaryllis are, in reality, four modified leaves that enclose the future flower and will disintegrate as the plant grows.

THE LILY

Tulip and narcissus bulbs produce layers covered by an outer brown tunic that resembles the texture of paper. These layers encase the flower-to-be. The tulip bulb dies each year, but is immediately replaced by one or more small bulbs called offsets (or bulblets), formed next to the layers themselves.

The offsets will be ready to flower the following year, or several years later, depending on their size.

Lily bulbs and fritillary bulbs are also made up of scales, but they are not protected by a tunic.

THE NARCISSUS

The corm

Corms have the same function as bulbs, except that their principal bulk is not formed by scale-like leaves. Corms have a large basal surface that is used as a reservoir of energy. It is covered by several dry tunics and disappears at the end of each growing cycle, giving way to its bulblets. Gladioli, crocuses, erythroniums, freesias and crocosmias are some of the plants that corms produce.

THE CROCUS

Tuberous roots and rhizomes

Tuberous plants are characterized by thickish roots that increase in size or multiply each year, eventually forming new stems from plainly visible buds. The best-known tuber is the potato.

Among bulbous plants, the zantedeschia (calla lily), the caladium and the gloriosa represent true tubers.

Dahlias, eremurus and ranunculus all have tuberous roots. They display several bulges, of which the lower part is covered with little roots and the upper part, with buds. Tuberous begonias and cyclamens are generally classified within this group, but their storage compartments — or reserves — are somewhat different.

The rhizome is a special kind of stem that grows horizontally along the surface of the soil or just beneath the ground. It is fleshy, at times tuberous, and displays neither uniformity nor separation. Cannas, oxalis, trilliums and certain kinds of iris make up the rest of the rhizome category.

PARTS OF THE FLOWER

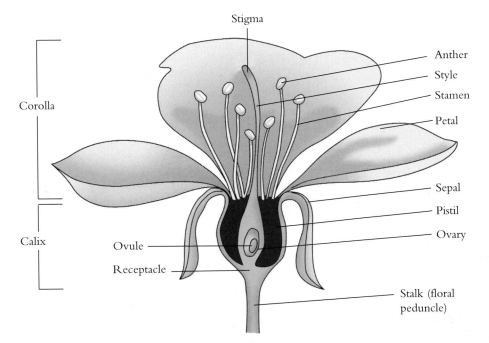

Stigma

Anther

Style

Stamen

Corolla

Petal

Sepal

Pistil

Ovary

Calix

Ovule

Receptacle

Stalk (floral peduncle)

PLANT HARDINESS ZONES

he correlation between climate zones and the hardiness of plant species is often a matter of debate.

Climate is one of the many essential factors to consider when cultivating plants. A number of bulbous plants are unable to withstand our winters, while the resistance of others depends upon just how cold temperatures can get. That is the reason plants are classified according to a range of climate zones.

Contrary to popular belief, the zones established by the United States Agriculture Department and those of the Research Branch of the Canadian Agriculture Department are almost identical.

	CANADA (IN CELSIUS)	UNITED STATES (IN FAHRENHEIT)
ZONE 1:	below –45°C	below –50°F
ZONE 2:	–45 to –40°C	–50 to –40°F
ZONE 3:	–40 to –34°C	–40 to –30°F
ZONE 4:	–34 to –29°C	–30 to –20°F
ZONE 5:	–29 to –23°C	–20 to –10°F
ZONE 6:	–23 to –16°C	–10 to 0°F
ZONE 7:	–16 to –12°C	0 to 10°F
ZONE 8:	–12 to –7°C	10 to 20°F
ZONE 9:	–7 to –1°C	20 to 30°F
ZONE 10:	–1 to 4°C	30 to 40°F

The hitch is that maps illustrating these areas can vary considerably as far as the area of the zones is concerned, and this often leads to confusion. The climate zone assigned to a particular plant may also differ from one publication to another. And although classifications are usually uniform in the reference books, there can occasionally be a few surprises in plant catalogues. For this reason, it's better to verify climate characteristics in official government listings.

Crocus chrysanthus, *an early species.*

The microclimate

The microclimate also makes a difference. Continuous snow cover during the winter plays an important role in the ability of several plants to survive.

Snow protects the ground from freezing, and works on the igloo principle. It has been observed, for example, that even in an outdoor temperature of -50°F (-50°C), if you insert a thermometer 2' (60 cm) under the snow, it will register a temperature of 23°F (-5°C).

For this reason, certain plants that have difficulty surviving winters that are milder than Zone 5 will grow in Zone 4, which is actually colder but has a heavier snowfall.

Other factors can influence a plant's survival — its geographical location, the presence of a large body of water, and natural or artificial barriers that act as wind-breaks or allow snow to accumulate.

Galanthus nivalis, *snowdrop.*

International Bloembollen Centrum

20

Mulch

It goes without saying that providing winter protection, such as a thick covering of mulch that prevents the ground from freezing, or a canvas or burlap cloth that reduces the temperature range, is an effective way to protect fragile plants from severe cold.

Farther south, heat can trigger adverse conditions. If the climate is too mild to permit certain bulbous plants to lie dormant, they will never flower.

Drainage conditions are just as important. Water accumulation in the ground over the winter months will cause many bulbs to die.

I've referred to a number of specialized studies to ascertain the hardiness of the plants described in this book, but I've also relied on the practical experiences of my own collaborators.

Hardy bulbs

How do tulip bulbs manage to survive the winter? The answer is genetics. The tuberous roots of dahlias and cannas cannot withstand frost, because they are not adapted to the cold environment. The tulip, on the other hand, has a process of acclimatization that kicks in once the temperature drops to 39°F (4°C).

The tulip bulb's cells are bathed in an extracellular liquid that freezes as the temperature falls. During the adaptation process, water is displaced across the cellular wall, so that the colder it gets, the greater the concentration of mineral salts inside the cell. It becomes a kind of antifreeze. The same thing happens with the enzymes and various proteins designed to protect the bulb throughout the winter.

Life goes on

The frost-resistant threshold has its limits, however. If the temperature dips down too low, ice crystals grow increasingly large and finally penetrate the cell wall of the bulb, causing it to die.

The same phenomenon applies when the flower stem starts to shoot during a milder than usual autumn or in the case of bulbous plants, such as certain muscaris, that produce leaves in the fall.

During the winter, continuous exchanges of gas occur between the bulb and the soil. If the ground is waterlogged, this process will be interrupted and the bulb will die. Hence the importance of good drainage.

A lethal temperature

Every plant species has its own individual built-in resistance factor. And each has its own lethal temperature. Here is a selection of lethal temperatures for bulbs.

Tulips	10°F	(-12°C)
Allium orophilum	-4°F	(-20°C)
Camassia cusickii	8.6°F	(-13°C)
Fritillaria camschatcencis	-4°F	(-20°C)
Lilium longiflorum	23°F	(-5°C)
Ornitholagum umbellatum	10°F	(-12°C)
Scilla siberica	10°F	(-12°C)

Summer-flowering bulbs are by definition regarded as tender bulbs. Experience shows that canna bulbs suffer damage even at 50°F (10°C), and tigridias and crocosmias at 35°F (2°C).

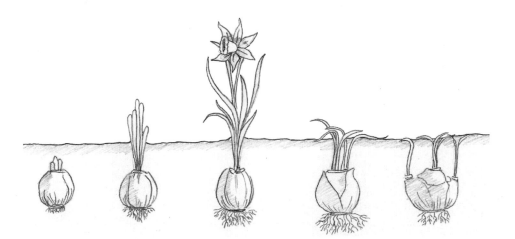

The evolution of a narcissus bulb during the growth period.

$\mathcal{G}$ROWING METHODS

$\mathcal{I}$t is relatively easy to grow bulbous plants. The special demands of each plant are described in the appropriate chapters, but in every case a few basic rules must be observed.

Bulbs like a light, deep soil, rich in organic material such as compost, which holds the moisture during the growing period. Or they can even tolerate a sandy soil. But it is absolutely essential that the soil be well drained in order to keep your plants happy and healthy. If there's too much clay in the soil composition, for example, it will need to be lightened by adding sand and compost.

At planting time, it's always better to group tulip bulbs together according to color and variety.

The zantedeschias (arum lily) or the calla lilies, some fritillaries and the colo-casia (elephant's ear) are among the exceptions to the rule, and do well in wet soil, at least during the growing season.

Fertilization

Bulbous plants make few demands as far as fertilization is concerned. But a dose of mineral salts from time to time will do them a world of good. It is advisable to use fertilizers specially designed for bulbous plants but, if need be, fertilizers low in nitrogen or a balanced formula such as 20-20-20 will do the trick.

Remember that in this case, the fertilizer includes 20 percent nitrogen, 20 percent phosphorus and 20 percent potassium. Nitrogen facilitates leaf growth but, if too high a dose is applied, growth will occur at the expense of flower production. Phosphorus stimulates root growth, while potassium encourages the storage of nutritive reserves in the roots, a vital process for all bulbs.

Propagation

Several bulbous plants seed themselves and increase their size naturally.

International Bloembollen Centrum

In Holland, flowering tulips are cut by machine after careful examination.

Internationaal Bloembollen Centrum

Tulip gathering for the florist trade is done by hand.

But they often need a helping hand. You can speed up the multiplication process by removing the offsets produced during the growth period. It's preferable to harvest them while the plant is dormant and to transplant the offsets at the appropriate time. Depending upon their size, the first flowering will take place either the following season or some years later.

The great majority of plants introduced in this book will also reproduce from seed. But that involves a real challenge and demands patience. Bear in mind also that the offspring of many hybrids and cultivars will not be identical to the parent plant.

Growing from seed: a long process

Some seed merchants sell bulbous plant seeds. If you want to go ahead and grow your own seedlings, you must use mature seeds. In some cases, they need to undergo a period of cold for several weeks in order to germinate. Most of the time, it is necessary to put the seeds in a pot and follow the development of the young plants for two or three years before transplanting them into a protected part of the garden. Then you'll have to wait until the bulb, corm or rhizome reaches a size sufficient for it to produce flowers.

The growing environment must be similar in composition to that where the seedlings were planted. It's a good idea to incorporate a little gravel and cover the surface with coarse sand, in order to facilitate drainage.

It goes without saying that in the mass production of bulbs a variety of sophisticated means of ensuring rapid propagation are employed. One can, for example, divide the basal plateau of the bulb so as to create several bulblets, especially with the amaryllis, hyacinth and daffodil. But these methods of multiplication need specialized techniques.

Naturalization

Many bulbous plants adapt easily to naturalization. All you need to do is put them in an appropriate spot and leave them to themselves.

Internationaal Bloembollen Centrum

Crocuses, especially the early arrivals, do well in grass.

Internationaal Bloembollen Centrum

Daffodils are a natural feature of many English parks.

If conditions of soil, temperature and light are satisfactory, bulbs will pro-liferate for years without special care other than an annual fertilizing, usually after blooming. In suitable conditions, certain daffodils can live and multiply for decades in the same place. That's also true for several tulip species.

Some plants, such as scillas, which do not grow very tall, spread easily across a lawn, forming magnificent carpets of flowers in springtime. Before going ahead with the first mowing, wait until the leaves wilt, or at least until the nec-essary reserves have been built up.

SPRING–FLOWERING BULBS
RECOMMENDED FOR NATURALIZATION

Anemone blanda	*Daffodil*: small-flowered
Allium: species and cultivars/varietals	*Daffodil*: large-flowered
Chionodoxa	*Puschkinia*
Crocus: large-flowered	*Scilla siberica*
Crocus: species	*Hyacinthoides*
Eranthis	*Tulipa kaufmanniana*
Fritillaria meleagris	*Tulipa fosteriana*
Galanthus nivalis	*Tulipa greigii*
Muscari armeniacum	Botanical tulips

Spring or fall?

Bulbous plants flower in the spring, summer or fall, according to the species. In areas with a more temperate climate, such as the Mediterranean basin, some bulbs — the ranunculus, for instance bloom even at the end of winter.

But the flowering period will also fluctuate depending on the gardener's activity.

By using a low-temperature treatment (or occasionally by heating) lasting several weeks, one can artificially induce the dormant period of a plant, and lead it to produce flowers outside its normal cycle. This is called "forcing" the plant.

In the Netherlands, for instance, millions of frozen lily bulbs are stored in warehouses throughout the year to meet florists' needs.

Some bulbous plants are not hardy enough for our climate: their bulbs freeze in wintertime. These are the tender bulbs. Begonias, dahlias and gladioli are members of this group. These species must therefore be planted in the spring. Flowering will occur during the summer and sometimes in the fall, generally later than in their natural environment. These bulbs must be dug up and kept in a cool place over the winter months so that they can be planted again the following spring.

Hardier bulbous plants are sold in the fall. They should be planted as soon as possible. In this case, perennial bulbs, rhizomes or tuberous roots will spend the winter in the earth without difficulty and a good number will flower in the spring. But there are some species that flower in the summer and even in the fall, in September or October — the autumn crocus (colchicum), for example, or *crocus sativus*, the saffron-producing flower.

Some hardy bulbs are also sold in the spring. They have lain dormant during their winter storage. Plant them as soon as you get them, but they will flower later than bulbs of the same species planted in the fall.

Forcing

Although it's relatively easy to force bulbs to flower outside the normal growing season, certain rules must be followed meticulously.

The great majority of bulbous plants need a period of dormancy during which they shed their leaves.

In the case of spring-flowering plants, dormancy occurs during the winter. For summer-flowering bulbs, a period of dryness or heat produces the same condition for dormancy. Note that all the while, the bulb's internal biological machinery remains at work

The length of the dormancy period varies with the plant. Plants commonly used for forcing purposes need a minimum rest period of 10 weeks, at a temperature from 35-48°F (2-9°C). If the period is too short or the temperature too high, the plant will not flower. The period of dormancy is preferably long rather than short. This period should last 13 weeks for hyacinths, 14 for iris, 15 for muscari (grape-hyacinth) and crocus, 16 for daffodils, and 15 to 17 weeks for tulips.

The method of proceeding is outlined in the chapter on tulips.

Double-page spread following: Many bulbous plants are easy to force.
Left to right: crocus, hyacinths, Greek anemones, muscaris, daffodils.

GIFT IDEAS!

The international bulb market amounts to hundreds of millions of dollars annually.

$\mathscr{A}$N IMPORTANT WORLD MARKET

$\mathscr{T}$he international bulb market — a very considerable one — well exceeds a billion dollars every year.

The Netherlands dominates this trade. In 1997, it exported more than $900 million worth of bulbs to some 100 different countries. Most were sold for forcing purposes in order to supply the flower-growing market. Tulip bulbs make up nearly one-third of the Netherlands export market, with lily bulbs in second place.

Canada, the United States, South America and South Africa also produce bulbous plants on a large scale. And the market continues to grow.

Various daffodil species, forced in the author's home.

Pierre McCann, *La Presse*

Gardening enthusiasts in North America buy 1.6 billion bulbs annually. The popularity of most species is always on the rise. Moreover, in some markets, if sales of Dutch bulbs decline, the reason is often that local production has increased.

COMPARATIVE SALES

	UNITED STATES 1998–1999 (in millions)	CANADA 1998–1999 (in millions)
Tulipa	414.4	64.4
Gladiolus	220.3	19.5
Lilium	142.7	18.8
Iris	134.6	12.2
Narcissus	123.6	12.4
Crocus	105.6	12.0
Muscari	46.6	4.4
Freesia	34.1	1.7
Hyacinthus	38.7	5.5
Anemone	41.8	2.9
Allium	40.7	2.5
Acidanthera	34.2	0.5
Sparaxis	18.7	0.4
Oxalis	13.7	0.9
Chionodoxa	10.4	0.8
Dahlia	11.8	0.8
Scilla	9.0	1.1
Ixia	6.0	0.2
Puschkinia	7.5	0.4
Brodiaea	7.4	0.5
Amaryllis	5.0	0.5
Galanthus	2.9	0.8
Ranunculus	3.4	0.2
Ixiolirion	4.3	0.1
Begonia	3.0	0.2
Fritillaria	2.5	0.8
Crocosmia	2.9	0.1
Other species	3.0	0.4
	1488.8	165.0

What to buy

When you buy bulbs, make sure they are tightly closed, undamaged and free from mould.

If the stem has begun to protrude, the bulb must be planted as quickly as possible. In the case of bulbs sold in the spring, look for any that have already sprouted or are showing stems, and put them in the fridge so as to slow down their metabolism while you wait for the right time to plant them outside.

Choose the plumpest bulbs. Dutch companies, for example, are not authorized to sell tulip bulbs that are less than 4" (10 cm) in circumference, at least as far as hybrids are concerned. In the majority of cases, however, bulbs measure 4¾" (12 cm) or more in circumference.

There is a big difference between a 4" (10 cm) bulb and a 4¾" (12 cm) bulb. The larger bulb will produce a larger flower on a taller stalk with fuller leaves. And it will be more expensive. Those are the best ones to use if you are interested in forcing your bulbs.

A guarantee

Unfortunately, wholesalers do not invariably respect the information printed on their packaging. The "Top Size" criterion, for example, doesn't necessarily mean that all the bulbs are maximum size. Examine those you want to buy to see if they are uniform in size. Some companies offer guarantees, and they are the most reliable.

If you want to be sure of getting bulbs that will produce flowers for several years, choose those that lend themselves to acclimatizing, a characteristic usually indicated on the package.

Catalogues often offer a wide selection. However, bear in mind that their prices are frequently higher — sometimes two or three times higher — than what nurseries or garden centers will charge for an equivalent item.

Allium
Bulbocodium
Camassia
Chionodoxa
Corydalis
Crocus
Eranthis
Eremurus
Fritillaria
Galanthus
Hyacinthoides
Hyacinthus
Ipheion
Iris
Ixiolirion
Leucojum
Muscari
Narcissus
Puschkinia
Scilla
Tulipa

Indigenous Plants

Arisaema
Erythronium
Lilium canadense
Polygonatum
Sanguinaria
Trillium

Spring

ALLIUM
Allium

Allium is the classical Latin name for garlic, and the origin of its cultivation is lost in the mists of time. The ancient Babylonians had a taste for it and as far back as 3000 B.C., the Egyptians dedicated a cult to the plant. It even had a monetary value in the land of the Pharaohs. A healthy slave, for example, was worth roughly seven kilos of garlic.

From time immemorial, folk medicine has attributed to garlic a host of therapeutic powers, some of which are still respected to this day. The word "garlic" may derive from a Celtic term meaning "strong," "spicy," or even "to cry."

Onions, chives and leeks belong to the lily family, a group that includes at least 700 species of perennial or biennial bulbous plants, of which a large number are now cultivated for decorative purposes. Several kinds exude the familiar garlicky odor when you rub their leaves, a scent attributable to a sulphur compound. Other varieties have a pleasant smell.

Alliums rarely go unnoticed and add a touch of magic to the flower bed. The flowers themselves form a pinkish-mauve globe atop a stalk capable of reaching more than three feet (1 m) in height. Some varieties, however, are parasol-shaped, not as tall, and have dainty pink, white or yellow flowers. They blend in well with perennials, while the smaller species are perfect for rock gardens.

Easy-to-grow seedlings

Alliums originated in the temperate regions of Central Asia, along the shores of the Mediterranean, but they can also be found in more northern regions, where most of the decorative species come from. Several species are native to North America, notably wild garlic (*A. tricoccum*) and a variety of chive (*A. schoenoprasum*) which is found in some riverside areas of the Gaspé and on Anticosti Island.

Once fully grown, the giant allium puts out lovely long-lasting flowers.

In their natural state, most alliums grow in dry, rocky, or mountainous environments. But in the garden they prefer a deep, well-drained, not too rich soil.

Alliums grow singly or in clumps. They need to be divided whenever they become too compact. Multiply by separating out the clumps or by transplanting the bulblets picked while the plant is dormant. You can also propagate by seed, but some seeds will take two years before germinating, and flowers will only appear two or three years after that.

Outstanding dried flowers

The leaves of several species — especially the largest — start turning yellow from the onset of flowering. But the leaves of the "Globemaster" cultivar stay green longer. Therefore it's a good idea to pick out a spot in the garden where the long floral stems can emerge without the leaves being too noticeable.

The leaves of most species grown for horticultural purposes disappear after the plant blooms. The bulb then becomes dormant until the spring. Alliums generally flower in May and June, but a few wait until July.

The range of colors extends from pink to red, passing through blue, purple, white and yellow. Flowering lasts for two or three weeks, occasionally a little longer, after which the inflorescence is adorned with small green fruit that produce lovely dried decorations.

Plant the bulbs 4-6" (10-15 cm) deep — up to 8" (20 cm) if they are large. Leave 8-12" (20-30 cm) between the taller varieties of allium. But watch out! If the soil gets too wet at planting time, the bulbs may be spoiled. Alliums are sometimes affected by leaf-spotting, mildew and rust. Thrips can also be a nuisance.

The main producer countries are the Netherlands, Israel and Japan.

ALLIUM AFLATUNENSE

Origin: garden. Often classified as *A. hollandicum*.

Description: narrow leaves, 12-16" (30-40 cm) long. Stalk: 35-40" (90-100 cm), topped by a globe or sphere 3" (8 cm) in diameter. Flowers: about 50, star-shaped. The "Purple Sensation" cultivar is fuschia-colored.

Flowering period: end of May.

Cultivation: a rich, well-drained soil.

Hardiness: Zone 4.

Nectaroscordum siculum bulgaricum

Allium aflatunense "Purple Sensation"

ALLIUM BULGARICUM

Origin: south-eastern Europe, Turkey, Ukraine, Iran. Classified today as *Nectaroscordum siculum bulgaricum*.

Flowering period: mid-June.

Description: very narrow, linear leaves, attached to the base, 12-16" (30-40 cm) long; they exude a strong garlicky smell when rubbed. Stalk: 2-3' (60-90 cm). Flowers: 4-12" (10-30 cm), pendent, bell-shaped, ½" (1 cm) across. Color: whitish with pale red tones, green at the base.

Cultivation: sunny or partly shady location. Moderately fertile soil, well-drained and slightly moist. It will become overgrown if conditions are too favorable.

Hardiness: considered hardy in Zone 6, but sometimes winter-resistant in Zone 5, after planting. In more severe conditions, it will rapidly deteriorate.

41

ALLIUM CAERULEUM
Blue Globe Onion
Origin: Siberia, Turkestan.
Flowering period: late June.
Description: linear leaves 3" (8 cm) long, borne by the stalk. Stalk: 20-25" (50-60 cm), topped by a dense umbel, ¾-1¼" (2-3 cm) in diameter. Flowers: star-shaped, 12-20" (30-50 cm). Color: blue, distinct from other alliums.
Cultivation: grows on the steppes and in the salt marshes of its native habitat. Plant in regular soil, well-drained, even dry. The leaves fade as the plant flowers. Plants should be grown close together.
Hardiness: Zone 3.

Allium christophii

Allium caeruleum

ALLIUM CHRISTOPHII
Stars of Persia
Origin: central Asia, Turkey, Iran.
Description: narrow leaves attached to the base, 12-16" (30-40 cm) long, edged with small fibers. Stalk; 1-2' (30-60 cm), topped by an umbel, 4-8" (10-20 cm) in diameter. Flowers: up to 100, star-shaped, ¾-1¼" (2-3 cm) across. Color: purple, with shiny highlights.
Flowering period: June, early July.
Cultivation: sunny, warm location. Leaves fade after flowering. A good variety for cut flowers.

Cross-breeding between *A. christophii* and *A. giganteum* produced the "Lucille Ball" cultivar, which has a stalk 40" (100 cm) tall topped by a thick umbel containing about 50 star-

42

shaped flowers 2-3" (5-8 cm) in diameter. Color: deep lilac.

The "Globemaster" cultivar results from crossing *A. christophii* and *A. macleanii*. It has a striking violet-colored umbel up to 8" (20 cm) in diameter. Height: 35-40" (90-100 cm). Flowering lasts 3-4 weeks.

The "Mount Everest" cultivar is the offspring of *A. stipitatum* and *A. aflatunense*. Closely resembling "Globemaster," it has white flowers, but the stalk is barely 2' (60 cm) tall.
Hardiness: Zone 4. Cultivars may be more sensitive.

ALLIUM FLAVUM

Origin: southern Europe, Central and Western Asia.
Description: tubular leaves, 8" (20 cm) high and ¾" (2 cm) in diameter. Stalk: 8-12" (20-30 cm), topped by an uneven umbel. Flowers: up to 60, bell-shaped, pendent. Color: yellow but with a tendency to mutate, occasionally reddish, greenish or brownish.
Cultivation: similar to other alliums.
Flowering period: July.
Hardiness: Zone 4.

ALLIUM GIGANTEUM
Giant Allium
Origin: central Asia, Iran, Afghanistan.
Description: narrow leaves, 1-3'

(30-90 cm) long and 2-4" (5-10 cm) wide. The tips fade quickly.
Stalk: 32-80" (80-200 cm), but rarely exceeding 80" (150 cm) in our climate, topped by a large spherical umbel 4" (10 cm) in diameter, often containing hundreds of flowers.
Color: dark pink.
Flowering period: end of May, early June.
Cultivation: rich, well-drained soil. Sunny position. Excellent for cut flowers, which release a light scent. A number of taller cultivars are sometimes classified as *A. giganteum*.
Hardiness: Zone 5. Fragile in Zone 4.

Allium giganteum

Internationaal Bloembollen Centrum

Allium karataviense

ALLIUM KARATAVIENSE

Origin: central Asia.
Description: a short-stemmed allium with two or three leaves, 6-8" (15-20 cm) long and 4" (10 cm) wide, almost horizontal, with a reddish border. Stalk: 4-6" (10-15 cm), topped by a dense spherical umbel. Flowers: Sometimes more than 50 starry flowers. The petals twist after flowering. Color: pale pink.
Flowering period: end of May.
Cultivation: plant on the outside of a flower bed. A new cultivar called "Ivory Queen" produces ivory-white flowers, and the blooms last for nearly four weeks.
Hardiness: Zone 4.

ALLIUM MOLY

Golden Garlic, Lily Leek
Origin: south of France, Spain.
Description: narrow leaves, lancolate, ½"-1½" (1-3 cm) wide and 8-12" (20-30 cm) long. Spike: 4-12" (10-30 cm). Flowers: sometimes as many as 30, erect, 2" (5 cm) in diameter, creating an umbel. Color: bright yellow.
Flowering period: June.
Cultivation: regular soil, moist and well drained. Plant at the front of a flower bed. Sunny location, but does well in partly shady spot. Good cut flowers. Adapts easily to naturalization. One of my favorite alliums.
Hardiness: Zone 4.

ALLIUM ROSEUM

Origin: southern Europe, Turkey, North Africa.
Description: narrow, linear leaves, 4-12" (10-30 cm) long. Stalk: 4-24" (10-60 cm). Flowers: 2-10" (5-25 cm), bell-mouthed, forming an umbel. Color: pale pink.
Flowering period: June.
Cultivation: a fragile plant, very attractive in a rock garden.
Hardiness: Zone 5.

Next page: Allium moly

Internationaal Bloembollen Centrum

ALLIUM SCHOENOPRASUM
Chive

Origin: North America, Asia, Europe.

Description: very narrow tubular leaves, erect, 12–14" (30–35 cm) long. Stalk: 4–24" (10–60 cm), topped by an umbel 1" (2.5 cm) across. Flowers: up to 30, bell-shaped. Color: pink, purple, some-times white.

Flowering period: May or June.

Cultivation: rich, well-drained soil, best in semi-shady spot. The chive is a variety of *fines herbes*, producing attractive flowers that can be made up into pretty, dry bouquets. The "Forescate" cultivar, with dark pink flowers, is very sturdy. It is 20" (50 cm) tall.

Hardiness: Zone 3.

Internationaal Bloembollen Centrum

Allium sphaerocephalum

ALLIUM SPHAEROCEPHALUM
Caucasian Allium

Origin: Europe, North Africa, Middle East.

Description: very narrow linear leaves, hollow, borne halfway up the stalk, 12" (30 cm) long. Stalk: 24" (60 cm). Flowers: Up to 40, dense, forming a nearly perfect sphere. Color: dark pink.

Flowering period: July, sometimes August if grown in the shade.

Cultivation: sunny or partially shady location. This is a superb alli-um, another of my favorites.

Hardiness: Zone 4.

Jardin botanique de Montréal

Allium schoenoprasum

46

ALLIUM TUBEROSUM
Garlic Chives

Origin: Southeast Asia.

Description: linear leaves, up to 14" (35 cm) high. Stalk: up to 20" (50 cm), topped by an umbel 2" (5 cm) in diameter. Flowers: numerous, star-shaped, fragrant. Color: white.

Flowering period: August.

Cultivation: widely cultivated in Asia as a vegetable. In Canada it is sold as a seedling plant and classified among *fines herbes*. Flowers should be cut after blooming, otherwise the plant quickly goes to seed, which spreads rapidly.

Hardiness: Zone 5, perhaps 4.

OTHER SPECIES

Allium atropurpureum: European origin. Flowers: numerous, umbellate, very deep red; stalk 35" (90 cm) tall. Zone 5, probably with protection.

Allium carinatum: sold as *A. pulchellum album*. Native to Europe. Stalk: 12–24" (30-60 cm). Flowers: Around 30, white and bell-shaped. Zone 3.

Allium oreophilum: pink allium. Sold as *A. ostrowskianum*. Native to Central Asia, Turkestan and the Caucasus. Linear leaves, 4-6" (10-15 cm) long. Stalk: up to 8" (20 cm). Flowers: upwards of 15, umbellate, purple. Flowers at end of May, early June. Zone 4.

Allium rosenbachianum: native to Central Asia. Flowers in June. Stalk up to 40" (100 cm) tall, topped by a dense sphere containing about 50 star-shaped flowers. Color: violet. Zone 5, probably 4.

Allium schubertii: native to the countries of the eastern Mediterranean, extending to Central Asia. Stalk 24" (60 cm) high. Huge umbel, up to 8" (20 cm) in diameter, occasionally wider, airy, containing about 50 elegant red flowers. Zone 4.

$\mathcal{B}$ULBOCODIUM

Bulbocodium

$\mathcal{B}$ulbocodiums are a relatively unfamiliar species. They are closely related to the colchicums (autumn crocus) and are every bit as spectacular. The flowers open in April or early May, sometimes just before their leaves begin to show. Their color ranges from bright pink to mauve or white, and they have six long spotted open petals, extending up to 3" (8 cm), emerging from the stalk, which forms a circular sheath. Six stamens with yellow anthers protrude rigidly from the center. The flowers last for a good while before fading. There are three narrow basal leaves, 6" (15 cm) long, concave at the top.

Although the plant's maximum height is only around 4" (10 cm), bulbocodium still puts on a dazzling display, especially if you have been clever enough to plant several bulbs together.

Mountain origins

Members of the lily family, bulbocodiums are native to the southern and eastern regions of Europe. Their scientific name means "capsule and bulb." There are two species: the one grown for horticultural purposes — *Bulbocodium vernum* — comes from the Alps and the Pyrenees, and extends all the way to Russia.

It will grow without effort in Zone 5, but some people find that it also does well in Zone 4.

Place the corms 4" (10 cm) deep in compost-rich, well-drained soil in a sunny position. The plant is well adapted to rock gardens. Multiply by seed or transplanting bulblets picked off during the summer.

Also called *Meadow Saffron*, the bulbocodium is largely disease- and insect-resistant.

Bulbocodium vernum

CAMASSIA

Camassia

alled Wild Hyacinth in England and Meadow Hyacinth in North America, camassias are easy to grow and will flower for a number of years.

They produce spikes of pretty blue star-shaped flowers and bloom later than some other bulbous plants.

The name *camassia* comes from the Native American *quamash*. In earlier times, their bulbs were a source of food for aboriginal people in the American West.

Camassias like deep soil, rich in humus or compost, well-drained but able to retain moisture. They will also grow in heavier, clayey soil as long as it is not constantly wet. The plant prefers a sunny position, away from hot, noonday exposure, but it will grow equally well in partial shade.

Propagate by separating the bulblets every three years in summer while the plant is dormant. They can also be grown from seed, which allows them to multiply easily.

Camassia is relatively free from disease and garden pests. The cut flowers last a long time in a vase.

Camassia cusickii

49

CAMASSIA QUAMASH
Quamash Camassia

Origin: western United States and Canada, southern British Columbia, Washington, California.

Flowering period: end of May, early June.

Description: narrow leaves, 12-16" (30-40 cm) long. Stalk: 16-24" (40-60 cm), topped by an inflorescence 4-8" (10-20 cm) long. Flowers: single, star-shaped with 6 flared petals, 1¼" (3 cm) in diameter. Flowers are numerous but scattered. Color: blue.

Cultivation: in its natural habitat *camassia quamash* grows in moist prairie areas and in conifer forests. Plant bulbs 4-6" (10-15 cm) deep. The "Orion" cultivar is dark blue. Plants are sometimes sold under their old name, *camassia esculenta*.

Hardiness: Zone 5, and with protection, Zone 4.

OTHER SPECIES
Camassia cusickii: stalk: 20-32" (50 to 80 cm). Flowers: pale blue, 1¼"-1½" (3-4 cm) in diameter. Zone 5, probably 4, if protected.
Camassia leichtlinii: stalk: 40"

(100 cm), ending in a spiky cluster of 30-40 scattered flowers. Color: White. The "Blue Danube" cultivar is violet. Zone 4, probably 3.

Jardin botanique de Montréal

Camassia leichtlinii

CHIONODOXA

Chionodoxa

Chionodoxas deserve to be better known. Their small blue or white flowers create veritable carpets of blossom over time.

They are among the very first bulbous plants to welcome the advent of spring. Their popular name — Glory-of-the-Snow — derives directly from the Greek roots of their scientific appellation.

Six species of chionodoxa come from Turkey, but others are found on the islands of Crete and Cyprus. Hardy by nature, they can survive in Zone 4. They are members of the lily family (*liliaceae*).

The plant's height barely exceeds 6" (15 cm), but at times reaches nearly twice that size, as in the case of *C. sardensis*. Seedling plants, however, flower early in the season and quickly lose their leaves, which makes them a good prospect for lawns. Growth will come to an end before it's time for the first mowing.

Fifteen flowers per stem

The blue, pink or white flowers with their clearly visible yellow anthers are spread out at the top of the spike. The number varies from 2 to 15.

The bulbs must be planted in the fall, 3-4" (8-10 cm) deep, in regular, well-drained soil in a sunny location.

Chionodoxas generally flower more abundantly during their second year after planting. The plant will then increase in size on condition that it is left to multiply naturally by seed, making sure that it gets a good dressing of compost during the autumn.

Propagate by dividing the clumps, or by picking off the bulblets and seedlings. Seedlings will take two or three years to flower.

Chionodoxas are seldom affected by disease or insects. The Netherlands is the world's principal producer.

CHIONODOXA FORBESII
Origin: Turkey.
Flowering period: April.
Description: linear basal leaves, growing in pairs, erect or spread out, 2½"-11" (6-28 cm) long. Stalk: 6-8" (15-20 cm), sometimes 30. Flowers: from 4-14, star-shaped. Color: bright blue, whitish center.

This species and its cultivars are often sold as *C. luciliae*. "Alba": white; "Pink Giant": pink with white center; "Blue Giant": blue with white center.
Hardiness: Zone 4, probably 3.

Other species
Chionodoxa luciliae: concave leaves, 2½"-8" (7-20 cm) long. Stalk: up to 6" (15 cm). Flowers: 2-3 per stem. Color: blue, white center. "Rosea": pink. Zone 3.
Chionodoxa sardensis: stalk: 4-8" (10-20 cm). Flowers: 4-12 per stem. Color: blue. Zone 5.

Internationaal Bloembollen Centrum

Chionodoxa luciliae

$\mathcal{C}$ORYDALIS
Corydalis

$\mathcal{M}$embers of the big poppy family, corydalis comprise at least 300 species of tuberous or rhizomatous herbaceous plants, that are usually considered to be perennials. Some, however, are classified as bulbous plants and sold as such.

That is the case with *Corydalis solida*, which grows from a spring-flowering tuber and is hardy in Zone 4.

It is a small plant occasionally reaching a height of 8-10" (20 or 25 cm). Its two or three alternate leaves are soft green, very denticulate, ferny and ornamental. They resemble the foliage of *Dicentra formosa* ("Luxuriant"), one of our longest-flowering perennials. The leaves disappear when the plant is dormant over the course of the summer.

The flower of *C. solida* is barely ¾" (2 cm) long, tapered and pink with a characteristic spur that is part of its charm. The plant's name comes from the Greek word *korydalis*, linking it to the appearance of the European crested lark.

Pretty clumps

In May, the plant produces a cluster containing 15-20 flowers. *C. solida* is well adapted to placement in a rock garden, in the undergrowth of bushes, or beside other spring plants taller than daffodils. Its leaves disappear fairly quickly after flowering.

Corydalis prefer a moderately fertile soil, rich in moisture-retaining humus, and like a partially shady environment where they can stay cool during the summer dormant period.

Native to Northern Europe, the tuberous *C. solida* will soon form pretty clumps of flowers if placed in a suitable spot. It seeds itself naturally. You can also divide the tubers at the end of summer, although it's preferable to leave them where they are for a few years.

Plant the bulbs 3-4" (8-10 cm) deep as soon as possible after purchase because they tend to dry out rapidly.

Internationaal Bloembollen Centrum

Corydalis solida

Some indigenous species

Two species of indigenous corydalis are found North America, and at least four other species, as well as their cultivars, are used in the garden.

Hardy in Zone 5, *C. cava* flowers in May and produces violet, pinkish or white flowers. If left undisturbed, the plant will form lovely colonies of bright blossom.

Widespread throughout Europe, *C. lutea* produces yellow flowers over a long period, sometimes lasting all summer. This rhizomatous corydalis, hardy in Zone 4, is obtainable in the northern United States and Canada as seedling plants.

The "Blue China" and "Blue Panda" corydalis belong to the species, *C. flexuosa*, and are often sold in nurseries as seedlings, producing blue flowers. They like a shady habitat. Flowering can last for a number of weeks, from the end of May until the beginning of July. However, these plants are barely hardy enough to withstand the rigors of a Zone 5 climate without winter protection. They are not considered either bulbous or rhizomatous plants.

Corydalis are susceptible to mildew if their location is too wet. Garden slugs also enjoy their foliage.

CROCUS

Crocus

Crocuses are coaxed out by the first rays of April sunshine — an annual miracle! They are less frail than they look, and can easily cope with the sudden changes that springtime weather brings in its wake.

Members of the iris family, they are small corm plants endowed with brilliant flowers, all the more showy if planted together in clumps. They're also hardy and can resist winter conditions in Zone 3.

Their popular name derives from *Crocus sativus,* the plant from which saffron is extracted. There are some 800 species and many cultivars. Crocuses are native to several regions around the globe, from central and southern Europe to central Asia, passing through North Africa and the Middle East. In their natural environment, they thrive in a host of different habitats, notably grasslands, woods and coastal areas.

An underground stalk

Crocus leaves, numbering from 2 to 10, are linear, threadlike, green, sometimes decorated with a silvery line down the center — like a tick of approval — on the back of the leaf. The leaves are unobtrusive by nature and appear at the same time as, or after, flowering, at least in species that bloom in the spring.

The underground stalk is invisible, and the flowers (up to four or more) emerge from inside a kind of sheath borne on a stem that continues to grow after flowering. Shaped like wine glasses, the flowers have six petals, ¾-2" (2-5 cm) long, in a very wide range of colors.

Crocuses are very easy to cultivate. They are quite content in a light, moist regular soil with adequate drainage and in a sunny or partly shady position where they can benefit from four hours of sunshine a day.

Planting with a hammer

Plant the corm 1½-3" (4-8 cm) deep. Its clawlike roots will help it to settle down gradually to an ideal depth.

As they usually flower early and the leaves disappear quite rapidly, crocuses will adapt to a variety of garden situations, rock gardens being a specially suitable spot. You can also plant them in the grass in thickly clustered groups, 1-1½" (2-3 cm) apart and 2" (4 cm) deep. The grass acts as an insulating carpet during the winter.

A simple method is to take a hammer and strike the ground sharply in order to make a small hole. All you need to do then is place the corm at the bottom of the hole. Next, spread a light composting material over the holes with a leaf-rake so that each corm is well covered. For the best effect, each plant grouping should contain crocuses of uniform color

It's important to check the soil level before planting. Any depression in the earth is liable to fill up with water during the cold season. If this happens, the corms will suffocate and rot.

The early varieties are best suited to lawns, since they have time to build up their reserves before the grass needs to be cut for the first time. And even if their leaves are shorter after the mower has passed over them, they will continue to fulfil their role until fading away. In dry periods, if the leaves are fully grown, you will need to water the lawn to keep the plants from rapidly deteriorating.

Predators at work

Crocuses are easy to force, especially the cultivars of *C. vernus*. Just plant the corms in a pot and put them in a cold place 36°-49°F (2°-9°C) for 15 weeks. If the dormant period is too short, the flowers will not bloom. Next put the pot at room temperature — but on the cool side, if possible — near a window, for example.

Multiply by separating the corms while they are dormant, or by dividing the plant colonies when they are thick enough. They can also be seeded. Some species seed themselves naturally.

Crocuses are a great temptation to a host of small animals. Squirrels, mice and field mice eat the corms, and in the spring, groundhogs, white-tailed rabbits and squirrels enjoy nibbling on the shoots, which are often the first plants they can make a meal of.

Crocuses are also susceptible to a number of diseases and, when corms are stored, they may rot. So it is always best to plant them without delay.

The Netherlands is first among crocus-producing countries.

Crocuses growing in a lawn.

Internationaal Bloembollen Centrum

CROCUS ANCYRENSIS
Origin: Turkey.
Flowering period: April.
Description: as many as 6 very narrow leaves, shorter than the flowers. Flowers: 1-3. Color: bright yellow. Height: 2" (5 cm). Species sometimes sold by the cultivar name "Golden Bunch," bright yellow, often producing 5 or more flowers per corm. This is the earliest crocus.

CROCUS CHRYSANTHUS
Origin: Turkey, the Balkans.
Description: 3-7 very narrow leaves, appearing at the same time as the fragrant flowers (from 1 to 4). Color: yellow or golden, but the exterior of the petals is often streaked with maroon. Height: 2" (5 cm). There are a number of varieties that

Crocus chrysanthus *"Blue Pearl"*

are often 3" (7 cm) high. They are sometimes referred to as Snow Crocuses. "Advance": yellow inside, violet outside; "Blue Pearl": pale blue on the inside, the outside lined with violet; "Cream Beauty": white interior, yellowish, greenish center; "Eyecatcher": greyish interior, purple exterior; "Gypsy Girl": yellow interior, exterior daubed with maroon, very pretty; "Princess Beatrix": whitish interior, blue exterior, yellow base.

CROCUS TOMMASINIANUS
Origin: Hungary, Bulgaria.
Description: 3-4 narrow leaves. Flowers: one or two. Color: lilac, mauve or violet. Height: 3-4" (8-10 cm). "Albus": white;

Crocus chrysanthus *"Cream Beauty"*

"Roseus": dark pink; "Ruby Giant": purple, almost violet.

Crocus tommasinianus *"Ruby Giant"*

Crocus vernus *"Pickwick"*

CROCUS VERNUS

Origin: Spain, Italy, Eastern Europe.

Flowering period: April, early May, later than other species.

Description: 2-4 leaves. Flower: one only. Color: white with purple tones. Height: 4-6" (10-15 cm). Several cultivars exist, often sold as large-flowered crocuses. "Flower Record": mauve; "Joan of Arc": white interior, exterior streaked with three fine violet lines; "Pickwick": numerous violet streaks on a white background, 6" (15 cm), very popular; "Queen of the Blues": blue lilac; "Vanguard": pale blue interior, greyish exterior, 6" (15 cm).

OTHER SPECIES

Crocus flavus: native to Greece, Turkey, the former Yugoslavia. As many as 5 flowers, yellow and orange-colored, fragrant. Height: 4" (10 cm).

Crocus fleischeiri: native to Turkey. Flowers: 1 or 2, open, star-shaped, white with yellow stamens, streaks of maroon at the base. Height: 2" (5 cm).

Crocus sieberi: native to Crete. Up to 3 flowers. The best known cultivars are "Bowles White" with white petals, orange stamens and throat; "Tri-color": petals marked by three distinctive streaks — lilac, white and gold.

Crocus versicolor: native to France, Italy, Morocco. 1-2 flowers: "Picturatus": white interior, exterior marked by violet traces. Zone 4.

Internationaal Bloembollen Centrum

Internationaal Bloembollen Centrum

ℰRANTHIS

Eranthis

ℰ ranthis is one of the earliest-blooming spring flowers. Its early flowering is contained even in its name, which comes from two Greek roots meaning "spring flower." When the ground is still colorless and bare, bright yellow patches of eranthis bring it to life.

It is also known as winter aconite or hellebore, a rare perennial that is one of our earliest-flowering plants (April).

Cultivated in Europe since the end of the fifteenth century, hellebore grows from a small tuber. It is a fragile, tiny plant scarcely 2" (5 cm) high, with delicate, denticulate leaves similar to the ranunculi that belong to the same family. Its solitary flower emerges from the center of a pretty ruff of leaves.

Native to Asia and Southern Europe, it is acclimatized in Northern Europe and North America.

Rapid growth

In their natural environment, aconites grow in moist woodlands. In the garden, they prefer a rich soil that holds moisture well, at least until summer begins. Under ideal conditions, the plants mature quickly.

Plant the tubers 3-4" (8-10 cm) deep, in sufficient quantities to get a striking result. It's a good idea to let them soak overnight before putting them in the ground. If they are dehydrated, they will not germinate.

It's possible to reproduce eranthis from seed. Under ideal conditions, they will produce flowers in three years. After flowering, clumps of a reasonable size can be divided once the leaves have disappeared.

Eranthis are seldom affected by disease or insects. Commercial production is concentrated in Turkey and the Netherlands.

ERANTHIS HYEMALIS
Eranthis, Hellebore
Origin: Southern France and Bulgaria.
Flowering period: April.
Description: delicately cut basal leaves, 3 to a stalk, attached right at the base, forming a ruff or whorl under the flower. Stalk: 2-3" (5-8 cm). Flower: single, cup-shaped, 6 petals, stamens clearly visible, ½-¾" (1-2 cm) in diameter. Color: yellow.

Cultivation: the plant does well in shady rock gardens or in front of flower beds. It will also grow in sunny positions.
Hardiness: Zone 4.

OTHER SPECIES
Eranthis cilicica: native to Turkey, extending as far as Afghanistan. Bronze-colored flowers. Flower slightly larger, blooming later, towards the end of April. Uncommon. Zone 4.

Eranthis hyemalis, *an unappreciated beauty.*

International Bloembollen Centrum

EREMURUS

Desert Candle, Foxtail Lily

*J*ust imagine! A spike of flowers 40" (1 m) high, sitting at the top of a seemingly endless stalk. Eremurus are probably the most remarkable of all the bulbous plants.
Unfortunately, they are still not widely appreciated, even though they are easy enough to grow and hardier than you might expect.

In the spring, the narrow, erect leaves first form a rosette. Then, a naked stem emerges from the center of the plant and shoots up quickly — you can almost watch it grow! The upper part of the stalk is covered with small flowers attached at right angles to the main axis. The height of large species such as *E. robustus* and *E. himalaicus* will occasionally surpass 6' 8" (2 m). In my own garden, a few *E. himalaicus* have reached a height of 6' 10½" (211 cm). Amazing!

Flowering occurs at the beginning of June or a little later, depending on the species, and lasts from two to three weeks. Flowers at the base of the spike will bloom first; and their color varies according to the species and the hybrids. Cut flowers will stay fresh in a vase for at least a week, sometimes longer if the room is on the cool side.

Available in the fall and spring

Native to Central and Western Asia, the plant is usually reproduced by seed, even in commercial settings. In the Netherlands, the seeding process starts in mid-October. It takes at least three years to get an interesting bloom.

Still not widely known on this continent, eremurus are relatively expensive and often hard to find. In the Netherlands they are harvested late. That is why the tuberous roots, shaped rather like an octopus or large spider, are delivered to North American nurseries some weeks after more conventional bulbs.

Tubers should be planted immediately after purchase to avoid the risk of dehydration. Dried-out roots must be discarded, because they will not germinate.

Deliveries are also sometimes made in the spring. Since dormancy has occurred during cold weather, the roots can be put in the ground at the end of April or in May. They will flower towards the end of summer or the following spring.

Winter humidity is fatal

Eremurus require a rich, gritty soil, extremely well drained. Winter moisture can kill them.

In its natural setting, eremurus grows in rocky and sandy habitats, often semi-desert or grasslands, hence its name, "Desert Candle." In reference to its striking in reference to floral spike, British gardeners call eremurus the "Foxtail Lily." There are about 50 different species.

The root is fragile and must be planted carefully and gently 8-10" (20-25 cm) deep. Leave at least 24" (60 cm) between the larger species. Avoid walking around the immediate area because compacting the soil may harm the delicate roots and cause them to deteriorate.

Eremurus need full sun and should be placed at the back of the flower bed because they are so tall. Leaves disappear after flowering, but the spike will remain if it's not cut. Collect the seeds at the end of summer.

A layer of compost applied during the fall will help to fertilize and mulch the roots.

The leaves are occasionally invaded by slugs. Some people stake the larger stems although they are fairly wind-resistant to start with.

The Netherlands is the principal commercial grower; Israel produces cut flowers.

EREMURUS BUNGEI

Origin: central Asia, Pakistan, Iran.
Description: narrow, lance-shaped leaves, 14" (35 cm) high. Stalk: 35" (90 cm). A spiky cluster of flowers, 12" (30 cm) long over all. Color: bright yellow.
Flowering period: mid-June.
Cultivation: easy as pie. Also classified as *E. stenophyllus.*
Hardiness: Zone 5.

Eremurus bungei

EREMURUS HIMALAICUS

Origin: Afghanistan, Kashmir, northwest Himalayas.
Description: narrow, lance-shaped leaves 12" (30 cm) high. Stalk: sometimes taller than 80" (2 m). Flowers: clustered along a spike 35" (90 cm) in length. Color: white.

Flowering period: beginning of June.
Hardiness: Zone 5, Zone 4 with snow cover or other winter protection.

Eremurus himalaicus, 6' 10½" (211 cm) tall

EREMURUS X ISABELLINUS

Origin: garden. From a cross between *E. stenophyllus* and *E. olgae,* the *E. isabellinus* hybrid originates from the Shelford and Ruiter hybrids.
Description: At 60" (1.5 m), the Shelford hybrids are shorter than their Ruiter cousins, which can

64

measure up to 80" (2 m). *E. x isabelli-nus* is sometimes sold as such and has a stalk 60" (1.5 m) long. All produce flowers of greatly diverse colors depending on the variety: orange, pure white, pink, pale red, dark red and yellow. A few are dwarf varieties.

These hybrids are sold in packets containing several kinds of seed. On the other hand, the roots of some Shelford hybrids are occasionally sold by specialty nurseries.

Hardiness: Zone 5. Ruiter hybrids are resistant in Zone 4 with snow cover or winter protection.

Eremurus robustus

EREMURUS ROBUSTUS
Origin: Russia, Afghanistan.
Description: lance-shaped leaves with a rough border, 1½" (4 cm) wide and 28-48" (70-120 cm) high. Stalk: at times taller than 80" (200 cm). Flowers: arranged in a spike, very numerous, 35-40" (90-100 cm) long. Color: pink, yellow stamens.
Flowering period: early June.
Hardiness: Zone 5 and Zone 4 with snow cover or winter protection.

OTHER SPECIES
Eremurus stenophyllus: native to Central Asia. Narrow lance-shaped leaves. Stalk: up to 60" (1.5 m). Flowers borne along a spike up to 24" (60 cm) in length. Color: yellowish. Hardy in Zone 5 with protection.

Eremurus, *Ruiter hybrid*

FRITILLARIA

Fritillary

ritillaries make an impact or everyone. With their unusual appearance, their dazzling bell-shaped flowers — and, in certain cases, their aroma that only a skunk could love — how could it be otherwise?

They're also adaptable to a variety of situations. Some species such as *F. meleagris* are equally at home in the shade and in sunshine — even a humid environment — an exceptional characteristic for a bulbous plant.

About 100 species of fritillaria come from the temperate regions of the northern hemisphere, especially the Mediterranean basin, the mountains of southwest Asia or western North America.

The name derives from the Latin *fritillus,* "a dice-box," which refers to the squared — or checked — appearance of the flowers of *F. meleagris*. It is also sometimes called guinea fowl's egg, precisely because of its geometric markings. This particular species began appearing in gardens as far back as 1572.

Bulbs with scales

Fritillaries demand special attention, but your efforts will be rewarded when the flowers burst forth in a spectacular array of color the following spring.

They prefer a compost-rich soil, very well drained, but not too dry in summer. Planted either in full sun or partial shade, fritillaries need a generous amount of water while they're growing. So don't hold back when watering them.

After the plant has flowered, the leaves turn yellow and gradually disappear. Don't forget to take this into account at planting time, especially when dealing with some of the taller species such as *F. imperialis*, which is almost 3' (90 cm) tall.

Enclosed within two or more fleshy scales, fritillary bulbs are fragile and susceptible to dehydration. They should be planted as quickly as possible after purchase. Place them on their sides about 6" (15 cm) deep, so that water won't accumulate in hollow center of the bulb.

Fritillaria imperialis *"Lutea"*

Pierre McCann, *La Presse*

Fritillaries may not flower in the spring if conditions are unfavorable. The same thing may happen the year after the first flowering — especially in the case of *F. imperialis* — if the fall and spring seasons have been very dry.

Look out for the lily beetle!

Some writers advise leaving fritillary bulbs where they are for years on end, while others recommend digging them up carefully after the leaves have wilted towards the end of June, in order to transplant them in the fall.

The bulbs of *F. meleagris* and *F. imperialis* give off a faintly skunky odor, and *F. imperialis* continues to smell while it's growing. Unfortunately that *Eau de Mouffette* perfume won't keep the rodents away — contrary to popular opinion.

Commercial producers use different methods to multiply fritillaria: offset bulbs, bulb scales or cuttings, tissue culture and also seed. If you choose seed, you'll have to wait five or six years — even under ideal conditions — before getting your first flowers. Seeds from hybrids rarely produce flowers identical to the parent species.

Although diseases among fritillaries are relatively uncommon, a brand new predator has turned up in the northern parts of our continent during the past few years, and has begun to wreak havoc, as many keen gardeners can attest. It's the lily beetle, a tiny red beastie that has added fritillaries to its regular diet. In my garden no plant species has managed to escape its unwelcome attentions. So be on the lookout in your own backyard. It will take several doses of pesticide to get rid of this insect. It's a lot of work but your lilies will be grateful.

The Netherlands exports the lion's share, though Turkey produces *F. persica* in substantial quantities.

FRITILLARIA IMPERIALIS
Crown Imperial

Origin: From Turkey to Kashmir, throughout Asia.

Description: narrow, alternate, lance-shaped leaves, 2½-6½" (6-18 cm). Stalk: 20-56" (50-140 cm). Flowers: 2½" (6 cm) long, numbering 3-12, emerging from a cap-like bract of small green leaves at the top of the plant, giving it the appearance of a pineapple. Color: orange, pale to dark red. The "Lutea" cultivar is bright yellow.

Flowering period: mid-June.

Fritillaria imperialis *"Rubra"*

Pierre McCann, *La Presse*

Cultivation: See introductory text. F. imperialis comprises several hybrids, including "Aureomarginata," whose leaves are edged in cream or yellow. It produces orange flowers. Make a note also of "Crown on Crown," with pairs of orange flowers one over the other; "Sulphurino": pale orange; "Rubra Maxima": dark orange; "Slagswaard" produces about a dozen flowers, at times more, on a stem reaching 56" (1.4 m) high. It has been cultivated since 1771.

The cultivars *F. imperialis* "Lutea" and "Lutea Maxima" produce yellow flowers. The latter is hardier than its cousin. Both are magnificent.

Hardiness: Zone 4.

Internationaal Bloembollen Centrum

Fritillaria imperialis *"Lutea"*

Pierre McCann, *La Presse*

Fritillaria meleagris

FRITILLARIA MELEAGRIS
Snake's Head Fritillary
Origin: Europe, from the British Isles to Russia.
Description: narrow, linear, alternate leaves, 2¹⁄₂-6" (6-15 cm) high. Stalk: 6-12" (15-30 cm). Flower: usually solitary, occasionally in pairs. Color: creamy white, purple, violet, greenish.
Flowering period: mid-May.
Cultivation: straightforward. This species likes moist locations, either in sun or half-shade. It acclimatizes easily, growing without difficulty year after year. But its flowers become abundant only after the start of the

second spring after planting. In its natural state, this fritillary grows in rich soils that are vulnerable to spring flooding.
Hardiness: Zone 3.

FRITILLARIA MICHAILOVSKYI
Origin: Turkey.
Description: lance-shaped leaves 2-3½" (5-9 cm) long. Stalk: 4-8" (10-20 cm). One to four flowers, sometimes as many as seven. Color: very deep purple, almost brown, the top third of the petal splashed with yellow.

International Bloembollen Centrum

Fritillaria michailovskyi

70

Flowering period: end of May, early June.
Cultivation: easy. Prefers rocky soil. Excellent in rock gardens. Less tall, but displays flowers of great beauty.
Hardiness: Zone 4.

FRITILLARIA PALLIDIFLORA

Origin: Siberia, northwest China.
Description: alternate, lance-shaped leaves. Stalk: 4-16" (10-40 cm). Flowers: 1½" (4 cm) long, generally about 6. Color: creamy yellow.
Flowering period: early June. Cultivation: easy, in rich soil, containing peat moss if possible. Partial shade. Exudes a disagreeable odor but hardly noticeable from a distance.
Hardiness: Zone 3.

FRITILLARIA PERSICA

Origin: Southern Turkey, Middle East (Iran, Jordan, Israel).
Description: alternate, lance-shaped, perpendicular leaves, 3-6" (8-15 cm). Stalk: 20-32" (50-80 cm). Flowers: up to 30, very deep purple, occasionally with black glints.
Flowering period: June.
Cultivation: difficult. Plant in a position protected from the wind. Will not always produce the anticipated results. Probably sensitive to cold. Only *F. persica* "Adiyaman" is available for sale.
Hardiness: Zone 5.

OTHER SPECIES

Fritillaria camschatcensis: native to Alaska and northern Asia. Partial shade. Stalk: 6-12" (15-30 cm), at times twice that. Flowers: up to 8, bell-shaped, pendent. Color: almost black, but sometimes green or yellow. Flowering period: early June. Zone 4, probably 3.

Fritillaria pontica: native to Turkey, Greece, the former Yugoslavia. Partial shade. Stalk up to 18" (45 cm). A single flower, or in pairs, bell-shaped, 1½" (4 cm) long. Color: greenish, with yellow and brown tones at the tips of the petals. Zone 6, probably 5 with protection.

GALANTHUS
Snowdrop

*D*espite their charming name, snowdrops usually make their appearance towards mid-April after the snow has melted. And in some cases they come out a little later, at the same time as some crocuses, reticulated iris, and several other bulbous plants.

Galanthus produce tiny flowers, suspended from the bottom of a greenish ovary. They are formed by three long, open white petals whose tips are often dotted with green. There are three more smaller white petals on the inside, also decorated with one or two dark green spots, sometimes haloed in yellow. A real gem.

The two or three leaves are usually shorter than the stalk when the snowdrop blooms, but they will continue to grow.

Native to Western Europe, as far as the shores of Iran's Caspian Sea, galanthus owe their name to a Greek word meaning "flower" and "milk." They are bulbous plants of the amaryllis family, and include around 15 species. Many cultivars are sold commercially under their own names.

Squirrels turn up their noses

Snowdrops like sunny or partly shady places, under the trees, as well as a compost-rich, moist but well-drained soil.

Susceptible to dehydration, the bulbs are planted in early autumn, 3-4" (8-10 cm) deep. Some people may develop skin irritations after handling galanthus bulbs. In fact, every part of this plant is toxic, for humans as well as animals. And that's why squirrels avoid them.

Snowdrops form natural clumps from their bulblets, but you can also propagate them by division or by transplanting the bulblets after flowering is over, when the leaves are still green. Patient gardeners use seed, but they'll have to wait at least four years before a single flower appears.

Galanthus are generally free from disease and insect problems.

GALANTHUS ELWESII

Origin: The Balkans, Turkey.
Flowering period: April.
Description: leaves very narrow at the base, then a little wider, 3-3½" (7-9 cm) long when the plant flowers, up to 12" (30 cm) later. Stalk: 4" (10 cm) at flowering but growing taller afterward. Flowers: scented, white, larger than those of the best-known species, *G. nivalis.* Color: white.
Cultivation: sunny location. Sold commercially as "Giant Snowdrop."
Hardiness: Zone 4, probably 3.

GALANTHUS NIVALIS

Snowdrop

Origin: Europe, from Spain to Ukraine.
Flowering period: April, early May.
Description: very narrow linear leaves, 3-4" (8-10 cm) at flowering, up to 6" (15 cm) later. Stalk: 4" (10 cm). Flowers: lightly scented, white.
Cultivation: easy. "Flore Pleno" or "Plenus": double flowers, but not as pretty as the original species; "Sandersii": yellow ovary, inner petals covered with yellow; "S. Arnott" or "Sam Arnott": rounded petals, large white flower, very fragrant; robust.
Hardiness: Zone 3.

Internationaal Bloembollen Centrum

Galanthus nivalis

YACINTHOIDES

Spanish Hyacinth

yacinthoides are prolific, prefer the shade, grow in ordinary soil — even if it is wet and heavy — and their flowering period lasts for three weeks. Spanish hyacinths are a springtime marvel. Unfortunately, a good deal of confusion still prevails in the trade as to their classification, and they are often sold under a variety of names: Endymion, for instance, or Scilla, whose close relatives they are. They are also commonly called Bluebell, English Bluebell, Spanish Bluebell and, occasionally, Wood Hyacinth.

There are four species of *hyacinthus*, all native to the Mediterranean basin.

A rock-garden plant

These members of the lily family adapt nicely to rock gardens, and look best at the front of a flower bed. It's a good idea to cut the flowers after they've bloomed. Multiply by separating the bulblets. Hyacinths are used as cut flowers even though they barely exceed 12" (30 cm) in height.

Plant bulbs in the fall, 3-4" (8-10 cm) deep. The greater the number of bulbs you plant closely together, the more striking the effect will be.

The plant is seldom affected by disease or insects. Commercial production is concentrated in the Netherlands.

Hyacinthoides hispanica

Hyacinthoides hispanica

HYACINTHOIDES HISPANICA
Spanish Hyacinth
Origin: Spain, Portugal, North Africa. Sometimes sold as *Scilla campanulata*.
Flowering period: mid–May.
Description: 5 or 6 narrow, linear leaves, usually erect, 8–16" (20–40 cm). Stalk: 8–12" (20–30 cm). Flowers: clusters of 15–20 bell-shaped flowers, petals bent backward. Color: blue.
Cultivation: easy. Will do best in partial shade under trees, but will also grow in sunny positions, though colors will be less vivid. The plant hybridizes easily with its cousin, *H. non-scripta*. Several cultivars are available: "Alba": white; "Donau" or "Danube": dark blue, lush flow-

ers; "Excelsior": pale blue with a dark line at the center of the petal; "La Grandesse": pure white; "Queen of the Pinks": pink; "Rosabella": pale pink; "Rose": pink, tinged with violet; "White City": white.
Hardiness: Zone 4.

HYACINTHOIDES NON–SCRIPTA
Bluebell
Origin: western Europe.
Flowering period: mid–May.
Description: numerous linear leaves, 8–18" (20–45 cm) long. Stalk: 8–16" (20–40 cm). Flowers: 6–16, tubular, bell-shaped, petals sharply recurved at the tips. Color: blue.
Cultivation: easy. The plant naturalizes without effort in woods or between shrubs and bushes.
Hardiness: Zone 4.

Hyacinthoides non-scripta *"Delight"*

$\mathcal{H}$YACINTHUS
Hyacinth

$\mathcal{H}$yacinths are admired for their vivid coloring and heady fragrance. In the older days it was said that iinhaling their aroma would cure certain illnesses.

The story of the hyacinth's goes back to classical antiquity.

According to a legend from Homer's time, Hyakinthos was a beautiful youth, beloved of Apollo. When the Apollo accidentally killed him with a discus, he caused the flower of the same name to spring from Hyakinthos' blood.

Hyacinths are members of the lily family. There are just four species, but the varieties grown today are all descended from *H. orientalis*, a plant native to Turkey, Syria and Lebanon. In their natural habitat they grow in rocky areas, often on cliffs or in the mountains, at altitudes of more than 8200 feet (2500 meters).

Harvested in Turkey, hyacinths first arrived in Western Europe in 1562. Botanists quickly began the cross-breeding process. The flower eventually provoked the same passions that the tulip had aroused, reaching such frantic heights that people were willing to pay the price of a house just to acquire a handful of rare bulbs.

Now, of course, the hyacinth is no longer a rarity and you can find dozens of cultivars on the market.

A delicate plant

Hyacinths have 4-6 rather fleshy, lance-shaped, gently curving, linear leaves 6-14" (15-35 cm) long. The stalk of some cultivars can reach a height of 6" (30 cm) and often bears as many as 40 single, bell-shaped, fragrant flowers with outward-curving petals. Some cultivars produce double flowers: "Ben Nevis," ivory white and "Hollyhock," red. The Multiflora group, including "Multiflora White," white, and "Borah," blue, produce multiple stems.

In our climate bulbs should be planted in a sunny position, 6-8" (15-20 cm) deep, in well-drained regular soil. Hyacinth bulbs are not frost-hardy: it's best to cover them with a mulch if winter temperatures fall below 14°F (-10°C). If the bulb is exposed at 25°F (4°C), it will be damaged.

Because they are delicate, hyacinth bulbs will degenerate rather quickly in Zone 5 if unprotected. By the same token, the second flowering will be far less abundant. In Zone 4, on the other hand, with snow cover, a number of gardeners have obtained even more flowers two years after the initial planting. Cut the flowers after they've bloomed to keep fruit from forming.

Hyacinthus *"Hollyhock"*

International Bloembollen Centrum

Allergy warning

Multiply bulbs by removing and transplanting the bulblets. Commercial producers use a special technique to slice the bulb.

Some people experience an allergic reaction after contact with hyacinth bulbs. If the bulb is too dry, its scales will crack, releasing oxalic acid, which can irritate the skin for a short time. If you're sensitive, wear surgical gloves or soak the bulbs in water before handling.

Forcing the bulbs is not difficult. Put them in a pot then store in the dark for 12 or 13 weeks, at a temperature of 45-50°F (7°-10°C). The potting soil should be kept moist but always well drained so that the roots can develop. As soon as growth begins, steadily increase the room temperature to 64-68°F (18-20°C). Start regular watering and put the plant in the daylight.

After the plant flowers and the leaves begin to fade, transplant the bulb outdoors. It will flower the following spring. Hyacinths that are forced hydroponically, on the other hand — that is, with their roots immersed in water — must be thrown away. These bulbs have been unable to store up sufficient reserves to produce a second flowering.

Hyacinths are vulnerable to a number of diseases, especially those produced commercially. In wet conditions the flowers may be affected by botrytis. The bulbs are also prone to rot.

The great majority of hyacinths are produced in the Netherlands and, on a smaller scale, in France and Japan. Exports exceed well over 100 million bulbs.

$\mathcal{I}$pheions are little known, but are appreciated for their large, pale to dark blue, star-shaped flowers. They are delicately scented with a fragrance some describe as minty but others equate more with honey. In any case, the leaves give off a garlicky odor when rubbed.

A dozen species or so come from South America. Controversy surrounds the origin of the flower's name, but for me it conjures up the asphodel, a Mediterranean plant whose stalk terminates in a spike of starry flowers. Ipheions are members of the lily family.

I. uniflorum, or Spring Starflower, is the most commonly cultivated species producing narrow linear leaves, erect but pendent at the tips, 8-10" (20-25 cm) long. The stalk is 8" (20 cm) tall, arching at the top, and bearing a single flower 1½" (4 cm) in diameter. The flower is a soft blue with a darker line across the center of the petals. The flowers close at dusk. The "Wisley Blue" cultivar is lilac blue.

Ipheion uniflorum

Grow them in pots

Ipheions like sun and a moderately fertile soil, rich in compost and well drained. They are considered Zone 6 plants but will grow in Zone 5 if protected with a mulch dressing during the winter. Plant bulbs at least 4" (10 cm) deep. Flowering occurs in May.

Ipheion uniflorum is native to Argentina and Uruguay. It is naturalized in France and Great Britain.

It can also be pot-grown indoors, and needs feeding once a month with a balanced fertilizer. Reduce watering during the winter while the plant is dormant. It will then continue to thrive for three or four years. The plant is largely free of disease, but slugs and aphids relish it for an occasional meal.

RIS

Iris

*I*ris cultivation is very ancient. A drawing of an iris is visible on the wall of an Egyptian temple built in 1450 B.C. The Greeks and Romans used the flower in the manufacture of perfume, as a cosmetic, and as a cure for certain illnesses.

The iris takes its name from Iris, the Greek goddess of the rainbow. In classical mythology Iris was the messenger of the gods, and of Juno in particular. According to legend, Iris descended the rainbow to the earth, and in her footsteps, flowers of all colors of the rainbow spring up.

Irises are an important feature of world horticulture. There are more than 300 species in the temperate regions of the northern hemisphere. But subspecies, hybrids and cultivars number in the thousands.

Irises are divided into two groups: those growing from rhizomes — such as the bearded iris, Siberian iris, Japanese iris and the variegated iris, to name only a few — and the bulbous irises.

Bulbous irises are in turn divided into three groups: the reticulatas, like *I. histrioides* and *I. danfordiae*; the Junos, like *J. bucharica* and *J. magnifica*, as well as the Dutch irises, the hybrids and cultivars issuing from the numerous species of the genus *xiphium*, which today are known as *Iris x hollandica*.

Though relatively small in number, bulbous irises play an important economic role to the tune of tens of millions of dollars annually. The Netherlands and the United States are the principal producers, but many other countries such as France, Israel and Japan make a contribution.

Dutch Iris

Dutch iris, or florists' iris, are not considered perennials in our climate. Some bulbs may endure a Zone 5 winter without difficulty and flower at the end of May, but they are the exceptions, unless you use a winter mulch.

On the other hand, some bulbs are heat-treated during the winter, then sold in the spring as summer-flowering plants.

These irises will thrive in well-drained, regular soil in a sunny position. The stalk is 1-2' (30-60 cm) high and the flower measures 3-3½" (7-9 cm) in diameter.

Iris reticulata

The irises in this group like regular (chalky where possible) well-drained soil in full sun.

They are 2-6" (5-15 cm) tall, shorter than other irises. They usually flower in early May, sometimes appearing through the snow in April, and flowers last just a few days. The diameter of the flowers barely exceeds 1¼-1½" (3-4 cm), but is sometimes twice that.

The leaves are narrow and erect, often longer than the stalk, but they don't shade the flowers.

Bulbs that are set down 2-4" (6-10 cm) deep can stay put for years. They will increase in size, even in Zone 4. After planting, give them a dose of a phosphorus-rich fertilizer. When flowering is over, spread a low-nitrogen fertilizer over the earth to encourage the growth of new flowers the following year.

Native to Turkey, *I. danfordiae* produces bright yellow flowers that have a greenish mark at the center of the petals. New bulbs must be planted annually, because the plant divides into numerous bulblets in the summer and they won't bloom the following year.

I. histrioides has a well-known hybrid that also originates in Turkey. It's called "Katherine Hodgkin." It produces a flower with whitish petals, the center of which is crossed by a splash of yellow. The edges are blue.

Many other *Iris reticulata* are also sold under their cultivar names. They include: "Cantab": pale blue with an orange marking at the center of the petal; "George": violet, up to 8 cm in diameter; "Hercules": very dark blue, orange markings; "Natasha": white, yellow markings. All these irises are hardy in Zone 4.

Iris reticulata

The Juno Iris

Iris in the Juno group have large, brightly colored pendent petals.

Native to Central Asia, *I. bucharica* has glossy leaves that can extend 8" (20 cm) in length. Its stalk is 8-12" (20-30 cm) tall, sometimes a little more, and is topped off by several yellow flowers. It blooms in May.

I. magnifica also produces very glossy curved leaves, about 6" (15 cm) long. The stalk, which can at times be 16" (40 cm) tall, bears 3-7 very pale blue flowers with a splash of yellow at the center of the petals. Native to Russia, it is a May bloomer. Hardy in Zone 4, these two iris grow nicely in a cool, even moist, location, providing that the soil is well drained, either in sun or partial shade. Their roots are particularly fragile. One must therefore divide them with care.

Try not to get water on the foliage, to avoid spoiling the leaves.

Iris are susceptible to a number of diseases, which is normal enough considering the huge range of species and varieties that the genus encompasses. Bulbous iris are not immune either, but as a general rule they are unaffected by disease or by insects. A number of fungal diseases can attack the *Iris reticulata* bulb, and may even destroy it.

Iris histrioides *'George'*

Jardin botanique de Montréal

82

ℐXIOLIRION

Ixiolirion

he name "ixiolirion" is a variation of "ixia," a starry-flowered plant which it resembles. Although not exactly a household name, ixioliri-ons can easily be found at garden centers that offer a wide selection of bulbs in the fall.

Members of the amaryllis family, ixiolirions produce up to a dozen violet flowers, 2" (5 cm) long, with more darkly streaked petals. Six yellow stamens spring from the center of the flower, adding contrast and charm. The flowers are grouped together in an umbel at the top of the stalk, which is 12-16" (30-40 cm) tall.

There are four native Asian species, which can be found growing at altitudes of 8850 feet (2700 m). Frequently sold as *I. montanum*, *I. tataricum* or Tartar Lily is the commonly sold bulbous species. It is hardy in Zone 5. Erect, lance-shaped leaves about 24" (60 cm) long.

Ixiolirion needs humus-rich soil, good drainage, and a warm, sunny position. Plant the bulb 4-6" (10-15 cm) deep. Flowering will occur late in the spring or early summer. The plant can be grown in a pot.

Propagate by separating the bulblets after the plant has bloomed, or by seed. Disease and pests are only minor problems .

Ixiolirion tataricum

ℒEUCOJUM
Snowflake

*S*nowflakes pop up early every spring.
They produce small, bell-shaped, delicate white flowers. At the tip of
each petal is an elegant green or yellow dab of color, as if a painter had
added it at the very last moment. They flower for a considerable period.

In addition to being tolerably hardy, leucojum — unusually for bulbous
plants — thrive in wet, even waterlogged, soil. A favorite habitat is the edge of
a pond. Long dry periods are unwelcome.

Leaves emerge from a case

Leucojum comes from a Greek word defining the white color of the flower.
Only two of the four species are used in Canadian gardens, *L. aestivum* and
L. vernum. All are close relatives of the snowdrop (*Galanthus*).

Members of the amaryllis family, snowflakes have 6–10 basal leaves that
emerge from a kind of case or sheath when they start to grow. They appear
before, or while, the plant is flowering
and can be as long as 20" (50 cm).

Leucojum multiply by seed or by
transplanting the offsets after the leaves
fade. Snowflakes are not disease-
prone, but now and again they will
attract the unwelcome attention of
slugs.

Leucojum vernum

Next page : Leucojum aestivum *"Gravetye Giant"*

LEUCOJUM AESTIVUM
Gravetye Giant

Origin: Europe, from Great Britain to Iran, by way of Ukraine and the Caucasus.

Flowering period: late April, early May.

Description: long basal leaves up to 20" (50 cm). Stalk: triangular, up to 24" (60 cm). Flowers: 2-8, pendent, attached to the stalk on a 2½" (6 cm) peduncle. Color: white, with a green spot at the tip of the petals.

Cultivation: rich clayey soil, moist, slightly water-resistant. The plant will tolerate stagnant water. Sun or partial shade. Plant bulbs thickly together, 3-4" (8-10 cm) deep. The "Gravetye" or "Gravetye Giant" variety has white flowers, is robust and hardy, and reaches a height of 30-35" (75-90 cm).

Hardiness: Zone 4.

LEUCOJUM VERNUM
Spring Snowflake

Origin: France, eastern and southern Europe.

Flowering period: May.

Description: waxy linear leaves, 8" (20 cm) long and ¾" (2 cm) wide. Stalk: sometimes in pairs, flattened, 8-12" (20-30 cm). Flowers: usually solitary, sometimes in pairs. Color: white with a green spot at the tip of the petals.

Cultivation: rich, moist soil, in partial shade, in wooded areas or under trees. Plant bulb 3-4" (8-10 cm) deep. The sub-species L. vernum carpathicum has a yellow spot at the tip of the petals. This species is sometimes called a snowdrop, thus confusing it with the real snowdrop, Galanthus nivalis. The stalk of the vagneri variety always bears two flowers. Height: 8" (20 cm).

Hardiness: Zone 4.

Internationaal Bloembollen Centrum

Leucojum aestivum

ᘇUSCARI

Muscari

ith delicate little blue bell-shaped flowers clustered in a spike atop their stalk, muscaris may appear fragile. But don't believe it.

They have a thick skin and can flower for years on end. The plants will increase in size over time and several species naturalize with ease, especially near big trees, around bushes, or in the grass.

Around members of the lily family, the arrangement of their flower head is very similar to the hyacinth, whose close cousins they are in fact. They are often called grape hyacinths.

Native to Mediterranean countries and southern Asia, their name comes from the Greek word for musk, because of the scent they produce. There are some 30 species, although some authorities mention twice that number.

The fleshy, slender leaves are scarce; fewer than a dozen or so. They look like blades of grass as they bend over, drawing attention to the flowers. The leaves of some species only show up in the fall and they easily withstand cold temperatures.

In summer, the leaves last well after the flowers have disappeared. Take that into account when placing them in a flower bed.

A bouquet of sterile flowers

Muscari flowers are borne like a cluster of pearls atop a leafless stalk that can be anywhere from 4-16" (10 to 40 cm) tall. The inflorescence itself is 1-6" (2-15 cm) long. Each inflorescence has a dozen bell-shaped or tubular flowers, narrow at the mouth and sometimes adorned with a pale border.

A number of species such as *M. latifolium* and *M. neglectum* carry an inflorescence with dark blue fertile flowers at the base with paler and smaller sterile flowers on the upper part.

These sterile flowers can also be found in little clumps atop completely white spikes. They are often oddly shaped — tufted, with slender, delicate flowers.

Muscari do quite well in regular soil but prefer well-drained, rich soil in full sun. Plant the bulbs at least 4-6" (10-15 cm) deep. And because they dry out easily, it's advisable to plant them as quickly as possible in the fall. The more thickly you plant them, the showier they'll be. Fertilize early in spring.

Easy to force

Muscari reproduce by offsets or division of the clumps in the summer after the leaves have wilted and the plant is resting. Commercial producers use offsets almost exclusively. It takes a year or two before a flower-producing bulb is obtained. You can also propagate by seed but even in favorable conditions it will take four or five years before flowers appear.

The plant is largely free of disease or infestation, but now and again thread worms may damage the bulbs.

Muscari are fairly easy to force so long as the bulbs have had the benefit of cold treatment between 35 and 48°F (2 and 9°C) for 15- to 16-week period. It's always a good idea to select the biggest bulbs.

Muscari bulb production is centered in the Netherlands.

Internationaal Bloembollen Centrum

Muscari armeniacum

MUSCARI ARMENIACUM
Origin: southeastern Europe as far as the Caucasus.
Description: linear leaves 12" (30 cm) long, appearing in the fall. Stalk: 6-8" (15-20 cm), inflorescence ¾-3" (2-8 cm) long. Flowers: bell-shaped. Color: dark blue, with a delicate white border. A few slightly paler flowers surmount the inflorescence.
Flowering period: May.
Cultivation: easy. The plant has been popular since the 1830s and many cultivars exist, though a number are extremely hard to find. "Album": white; "Blue Spike": double flowers, pale blue; "Cantab": robust, pale blue; "Early Giant": blue; "Fantasy Creation": double

Muscari armeniacum *"Fantasy Creation"*

flowers, pale blue, resembling the lilac; "Sky Blue": pale blue, white border.
Hardiness: Zone 3.

MUSCARI AZUREUM
Origin: Turkey.
Description: leaves curved at the tips, 2½-8" (6-20 cm) long. Stalk: 4-8" (10-20 cm) high. Flowers: bell-shaped. Color: sky-blue, with darker vertical markings.
Flowering period: early May.
Cultivation: easy. The "Album" cultivar produces white flowers.
Hardiness: Zone 3.

Muscari comosum *"Plumosum"*

MUSCARI BOTRYOIDES

Origin: central and southeastern Europe.

Description: leaves 2-10" (5-25 cm) long. Stalk: up to 12" (30 cm). Flowers: small, bell-shaped, fragrant. Color: bright blue, white border.

Flowering period: May.

Cultivation: easy. The "Album" cultivar has white flowers. "Superstar": blue, topped with pale blue flowers.

Hardiness: Zone 4.

Internationaal Bloembollen Centrum

Muscari latifolium, *a beauty!*

MUSCARI COMOSUM

Origin: Europe and Iran.

Description: leaves 6" (15 cm) long, some erect. Stalk: up to 16" (40 cm). Flowers: small, bell-shaped, perpendicular to the stalk, not numerous. Spike: 2½-8" (6-20 cm) tall, topped by a tuft of slender, fragrant, sterile flowers. Color: the little bell-like flowers are a pale violet, greenish at the base. Sterile flowers are dark violet.

Flowering period: end of May.

Cultivation: easy. The "Plumosum" cultivar is composed of sterile flowers, pinkish or mauve, slender and graceful, giving the plant a feathery look.

Hardiness: Zone 4.

MUSCARI LATIFOLIUM

Origin: southwest Asia.

Description: Leaves 6-8" (15-20 cm) long, often pendent. Stalk: 4-8" (10-20 cm). Spike: 1¼-2½" (3-6 cm). Color: dark violet. Topped by a tuft of sterile blue flowers.

Flowering period: mid-May.

Cultivation: easy. This is a splendid muscari, my favorite by far.

Hardiness: Zone 4.

MUSCARI NEGLECTUM

Origin: Europe, North Africa, Southwest Asia.

Description: leaves 2½"-16" (6-40 cm) long, often appearing in the fall. Stalk: 4-8" (10-20 cm). Spike of 1¼-2" (3-5 cm). Color: violet shading to black, white border. Topped by a tuft of sterile blue flowers.

Cultivation: easy. It has been grown for 400 years.

Hardiness: Zone 4.

NARCISSUS
Daffodil

or generations, daffodils have been synonymous with the spring, and their elegant beauty exerts an enduring fascination.

The naturalist Carl von Linné (Linnaeus) fell under their spell in the eighteenth century. As far as the Swedish botanist — father of modern scientific nomenclature — was concerned, they were the loveliest of all bulbous plants known at the time. So it was entirely appropriate to give them the name Narcissus, a figure in classical mythology renowned for his great beauty.

The nymph Echo fell deeply in love with Narcissus, but when it became clear that he preferred the hunt to her own charms, she grew increasingly upset. Calling upon the aid of a goddess, Echo planned her revenge. While Narcissus was quenching his thirst at a stream one day, he became so entranced by his own

Daffodils naturalized in a private park in England.

Internationaal Bloembollen Centrum

91

reflection that he could not tear himself away. Finally, worn out with fatigue, the youth fell into the water and drowned. Later, a magnificent flower appeared on the spot where the drama had unfolded.

A soothing effect

The original Greek name for the flower is less romantic. The term *narkissos* calls to mind the word, "torpor." Indeed, extract of narcissus was once used as a tranquillizer. Moreover, it used to be said that animals who ate the bulbs would be overcome by lethargy. Narcissi are toxic for humans, and, if ingested, can cause gastric complaints.

They belong to the amaryllis family. About 50 species come from the Mediterranean basin, and also from Western Asia, China and Japan.

In Egypt, under Roman rule, the flowers were grown commercially in great numbers. But it was not until the seventeenth century that the narcissus made its first appearance in the gardens of Europe. Today, there are literally thousands of cultivars, some 300 of which are widely sold.

A rather fragile daffodil

Daffodils are bulbous plants and produce a number of narrow, linear basal leaves, sometimes cylindrical and often erect.

The stalk is bare, topped by one or more flowers — sometimes as many as twenty. Each is formed by six large petals joined at the center, and shaped like a cup or trumpet. Fully grown, they produce a capsule containing a large number of seeds.

The majority of garden daffodils are cultivars hardy in Zones 3 and 4. That is not the case with the "true" daffodil, *Narcissus jonquilla*, a wild species native to Spain and Portugal, which is highly fragrant and has multiple yellow flowers. It is sometimes sold by catalogue and can be hardy in Zone 5 if protected by a thick blanket of mulch. But this daffodil has also produced a number of hybrids with multiple flowers that have proved themselves well able to withstand our winters — "Baby Moon," for example, whose flowers are completely yellow.

Beauty for decades

Daffodils grow in loose, regular soil, with plenty of compost, well-drained but able to retain moisture. If the earth is too clayey, lighten it with sand and compost because water accumulation will destroy the bulbs.

Narcissus jonquilla *"Sugarbush"*

The plant thrives in the sun but will also be content in partial shade. In this case, however, its longevity will be considerably reduced. Under ideal conditions daffodils live and multiply for years, even decades. In England they are used to naturalize and spread in broad colonies through public parks and lawns. This tradition is starting to be revived in North America. After blooming, keep the foliage for 4-6 weeks, time enough for the bulbs to build up their reserves in anticipation of the following spring. Then you can cut them at the same time as the grass.

Noseworthy

Before starting to plant, keep in mind the flowering periods of the different varieties to be used. Some bloom at the beginning of May, while others wait until early June. Theoretically, in places where the spring season is on the cool side, the late-blooming small-cupped daffodils will flower longer than the rest.

Plant the bulbs 6" (15 cm) deep during the autumn, even as late as December in some cases. I remember once planting bulbs 3" (7 cm) deep on December 26, while the frozen ground was covered with snow. They all bloomed in the spring. Nevertheless, it is preferable to plant early that roots will have a good chance to grow.

Add a special bulb fertilizer to the planting soil. Its effect will be more immediate than bonemeal or a mineral-based fertilizer.

The tips of the bulbs taper to a point, often called the "nose," each one corresponding to a future stem. Bulbs with only one nose are larger and more expensive. They will produce a stronger plant with more abundant flowers.

Easy to make part of your garden

When the flower buds appear in the spring, it's time to spread a little compost over the surface of the soil. After the flowering period is over, a potassium-rich fertilizer will help to ensure longer life for your daffodils.

The foliage often lasts for a good part of the summer, a feature that helps daffodils integrate within the flower bed, because the leaves turn yellow just at the time that the surrounding garden plants are abundant. You can also grow them in the lawn. And make a point of cutting off wilted leaves.

Propagate by division of the bulbs over the course of the summer after the leaves have faded. You can also try seed, but that involves a process lasting for a number of years, perhaps as many as nine. Bear in mind that cultivars do not produce offspring identical to their parents.

Daffodils make attractive cut flowers that last well in a vase. But don't mix them in with tulips because their stems exude a sticky substance that will shorten their neighbors' lives. On the other hand, if you place daffodils in water for 24 hours without cutting the stems, they will cohabit with your tulips on friendly terms.

English hybrids

Cross-breeding activity is concentrated in England, while the Netherlands produces the bulbs sold in North America. Americans bought 123 million daffodil bulbs in the fall of 1998; Canadians, 12 million. Worldwide, the five most popular varieties are (in the following order): "Carlton," "Ice Follies," "Minnow," "Tête à Tête" and "Dutch Master." In North America itself, the honors list is slightly different: "Ice Follies," "Dutch Master," "Salome," "Tête à Tête" and "Carlton."

Large-cupped daffodil "Flower Record"

Internationaal Bloembollen Centrum

Commercially grown daffodils are susceptible to a host of diseases; those grown in the garden have far less trouble.

On occasion the larvae of the daffodil bulb fly will hollow out the inside of the bulb and create an opportunity for rot to set in. Some threadworms also attack the bulbs, and a species of centipede can cause significant damage. During storage, crowds of plant lice or aphids may appear. If this happens, the affected bulbs must be thrown out immediately or disinfected with a pesticide containing malathion.

Forcing procedures

Daffodils are easy to force. Just place the bulbs side by side with the "nose" protruding a little from the surface of the potting soil. The pot should be at least 6" (15 cm) high to give the roots all the room they need to expand. Next, place the pot in an environment where the temperature varies between 35° and 48°F (2° and 9°C), for at least 14 weeks. If the bulbs are put in a cold room, make sure there's no fruit in the vicinity, because the ethylene released by the fruit will abort blooming.

As soon as the leaves reach a length of 4-6" (10-15 cm), you can put the plants in full daylight near a window so the air stays cool. But don't put them in direct sun right away.

Once forced, the daffodils can be transplanted to the flower bed. They will flower again either the following spring or in two years' time.

If you like, cut the flowers after they have bloomed. Then adopt normal plant maintenance procedures, fertilizing them regularly with a balanced formula. Stop watering as soon as the leaves yellow. Then transplant the dry bulbs in the garden toward the end of May rather than putting them into storage, because there's always the risk of dehydration if conditions are not adequately cool and humid.

Many varieties are suitable for forcing but some do better than others: in particular, "Carlton," "Dutch Master," "Golden Harvest," "Flower Record," and "February Gold."

"Paperwhite" narcissi, sold for indoor forcing, must be thrown away after use. They are not perennial in our climate.

One big family

Daffodils are divided into 13 categories.

1. Trumpet daffodils: one flower per stem; trumpet as long as or longer than the petals. The category is subdivided by color: white, yellow or three shades. "Dutch Master": yellow petals and trumpet, 16" (40 cm); "Chinese Coral": white petals, pink trumpet, 12" (30 cm); "King Alfred": yellow petals and trumpet, 18" (45 cm). Created in 1899, "King Alfred" is cultivated very little in the Netherlands. Yet it remains one of the most popular varieties in North America. There are similar, and prettier, varieties that can be bought instead: notably "Golden Harvest," "Yellow Sun," or "Dutch Master."

2. Large-cupped daffodils: one flower per stem; shaped like a funnel, the cup is more than one-third longer than the petals. Best known in this group is "Carlton": completely yellow, 18" (45 cm); "Flower Record": white petals, yellow cup with reddish border, 16" (40 cm); "Gentle Giant": yellowish petals, dark orange cup, curly border, 24" (60 cm).

Trumpet daffodil "Dutch Master"

Internationaal Bloembollen Centrum

3. Small-cupped daffodils: one flower per stem; cup only one-third the length of the petals. "Barrett Browning": white petals, dark orange cup, 16" (40 cm); "Birma": yellow petals, cup yellow at the center, dark orange border, 18" (45 cm); "Edna Earl": white petals, cup has yellow center, reddish border, 16" (40 cm). All three are magnificent.

Double daffodil "Tahiti"

Small-cupped daffodil "Birma"

4. Double-flowered daffodils: flower has more than 6 petals. Category subdivided according to the number of flowers borne by the stalk. "Petit Four": apricot-colored petals, orange cups, multiple and creased, 16" (40 cm); "Tahiti": yellow petals with orange tints, multiple cups with bright orange parts, 16" (40 cm); "Sir Winston Churchill": multiple flowers, fragrant, white petals, multiple cups with touches of yellow, 14" (35 cm).

5. Triandrus daffodils: retain the characteristics of one of the original parents, *N. triandrus*. Flowers pendent and usually multiple. "Thalia": white flowers, multiple, fragrant, 14"

Triandrus daffodil "Thalia"

(35 cm); "Petrel": white flowers, but the lower part of the petals is yellowish, multiple, 14" (35 cm); "Hawera": yellow flowers, multiple, fragrant, 6" (15 cm).

6. Cyclamineus daffodils: short-stemmed daffodils 8-10" (20-25 cm) descended from *N. cyclamineus*, flowers often single, petals upturning at the tips and a narrow trumpet. "Jack Snipe": pale yellow petals, bright yellow trumpet, long-blooming, 8" (20 cm). "February Gold": yellow flowers, large trumpet, early-blooming, 12" (30 cm); "Jetfire": yellow petals, long bright orange trumpet, 14" (35 cm).

Jonquilla daffodil "Quail"

Moon": small yellow flowers, 8" (20 cm); "Quail": yellow flowers, late blooming, 14" (35 cm); "Suzy": one or two fragrant flowers with orange petals and cup, 16" (40 cm).

8. Tazetta daffodils: descended from *N. tazetta*. Multiple flowers, 3-20 per stem, with a small, low cup. "Minnow": up to five early yellow flowers, 7" (18 cm); "Geranium": white petals, dark orange cup, 16" (40 cm); "Grand Soleil d'Or": several fragrant flowers with bright yellow petals and orange cup, 18" (45 cm). Used in forcing. These daffodils decline rapidly in the garden from one year to the next. In Zone 5, protect plants with a mulch.

Cyclamineus daffodil "Jack Snipe"

7. Jonquilla daffodils: descended from *N. jonquilla* and with similar characteristics. They carry from 1-5 fragrant yellow flowers per stem. Leaves usually cylindrical. "Baby

Tazetta daffodil "Geranium"

9. Poeticus daffodils: descended from *N. poeticus*. One flower per stem, petals are white and the cup yellow, decorated with a red border and green center. They are late-bloomers. "Actea": highly fragrant flowers, 16" (40 cm); "Como": fragrant, 12" (30 cm); "Poet's Way": fragrant, 16" (40 cm). Sometimes called the poets' daffodils, they flower later than the other varieties. Will also grow in fairly heavy soil.
10. Natural species and hybrids: this category includes all the wild

Poeticus daffodils "Actea," naturalized in a European park

Narcissus *"Rip van Winkle"*

narcissi. The "Rip van Winkle" hybrid *N. pumilus minor* is often classified with this group, though it actually belongs in Category 4. Its appearance is unique. Double petals, wavy, greenish-yellow, pointed out-

Narcissus bulbocodium

Split-corona daffodil "Cassata"

ward, 1½" (14 cm). Zone 5.

11. Split-corona ("Collar" or "orchid-flowered") daffodils: these *narcissi* have a slightly flattened cup, often torn or crumpled, resembling a second set of petals. Some have a collar- or butterfly-shaped cup. "Cassata": white flowers, 16" (40 cm) high, very large, up to 4" (10 cm) in diameter. "Rosado": pink flowers, 14" (35 cm). "Tricollet": white petals, distinctive cup shaped like a windmill blade, 14" (35 cm).

12. Other *narcissi*: these include

varieties that cannot otherwise be classified, including *N. bulbocodium,* with very delicate yellow cone-shaped flowers, 6" (15 cm) high. "Jumblie": recurved yellow petals, long, dark orange cylindrical trumpet, 8" (20 cm). Hardiness in Zone 5 is problematic, but will sometimes withstand its winters.

13. Narcissi identified by botanical names: *N. assoanus,* native to France and Spain, yellow petals, dark yellow cup, 2½-10" (7-25 cm) high. *N. asturiensis,* native to Portugal, greenish flowers, 2½-5" (7-14 cm) high; *N. serotinus,* native to the Mediterranean basin, white petals, dark orange cup, 5-12" (13-30 cm) high. *Narcissus asturiensis* is theoretically hardy in Zone 4, but very hard to find.

102

PUSCHKINIA
Puschkinia

Closely resembling dwarf hyacinths, puschkinias are actually related to scillas and chionodoxas. According to the Royal Horticultural Society, they are named for Count Apollosovich Mussin-Puschkin, a Russian chemist who brought them to Europe from a plant-collecting trip to the Caucasus.

There is a single species, *Puschkinia scilloides* (or striped squill), native to the Middle East, especially northern Iraq and Lebanon. Found in relatively harsh habitats, they form pretty clumps and need no special attention.

Puschkinias are members of the lily family; bearing two, sometimes three, narrow leaves, partially erect, growing from the base of the plant, about 6" (15 cm) long. The stalk is leafless, 4-6" (10-15 cm) tall, sometimes more.

Abundant blooms in dry ground

The floral spike contains 6-12 wide-mouthed, bell-shaped flowers, ¹/₂-2" (1-5 cm) in diameter and attached to the stem with a tiny peduncle.

Puschkinias are colored is a very pale blue with a darker streak at the center of the petals. The flowers of the *libanotica* variety are white, but smaller. The "Alba" cultivar has white flowers.

Puschkinias are not fussy plants and will grow in ordinary soil, either in full sun or partial shade. In fact, their flowers are more abundant in places where the earth gets drier as the summer goes on.

It is possible to reproduce by seed in the fall, as Dutch growers do, but it will take at least three years for the plant to bloom. Clumps can be divided or offsets transplanted at the end of summer when the bulb is dormant.

While insects are not a problem, puschkinias are prone to viral diseases, at least when commercially produced. In the garden, however, there is little to worry about.

Internationaal Bloembollen Centrum

Puschkinia libanotica *is a flower of great refinement.*

SCILLA
Scilla

Scillas are the first flowers to pop up from the grass, waving their little blue bells and signalling the arrival of spring.

Packed tightly together, they form entrancing floral carpets that gradually spread out as the years go by. There are some 90 species native to Europe, Asia and South Africa. They belong to the lily family. Because they are frost-hardy, the varieties grown in Canada and northern U.S.A. are of European origin.

There is some confusion among wholesalers as to their classification. Many are sold, quite incorrectly, as hyacinthoides, a totally separate species.

In the lawn

Garden-grown scillas are usually small: not more than 4-8" (10-20 cm) tall. They are ideal for rock gardens, naturalized over the lawn, or under trees. They can also be grown among shrubs and bushes.

While scillas are not temperamental, either about the kind of soil they grow in or the amount of sunlight they manage to get, their color will be brighter and their flowering last longer if they're put in partial shade. Plant bulbs in the autumn 3-4" (8-10 cm) deep, in rich well-drained soil. Pack them closely together for maximum effect.

Propagate by division of the clumps after the leaves have faded. Scillas are generally disease-free and insect-resistant. The Netherlands is the main producer.

SCILLA LITARDIERI

Origin: the former Yugoslavia.

Description: 3-6 linear, smooth, semi-erect leaves, ¾-2" (2-5 cm) long, narrow at each end,

Scilla siberica

appearing before blooming. Stalk: 2-8" (5-20 cm), topped by 3-35 flowers grouped in a thick conical spike. Flowers: starry, purplish-blue. Often sold as *S. amethystina*.

Hardiness: Zone 3.

SCILLA MISCHTSCHENKOANA

Origin: Iran, Georgia, Armenia, Russia.

Description: 3-5 linear leaves, 1½-4" (4-10 cm), which appear as the flower blooms. Stalk: sometimes 2 or 3, 2-4" (5-10 cm) tall, ending in a sparse cluster of 2-6 flowers. Flowers: Starry, pale blue with dark blue streak. Often sold as *S. tubergeniana*.

Hardiness: Zone 3.

Internationaal Bloembollen Centrum

A colony of Scilla mischtschenkoana

International Bloembollen Centrum

Scilla siberica *naturalizes easily.*

SCILLA SIBERICA
Siberian Squill
Origin: Iran, Russia, Ukraine, Turkey.
Description: 2-4 narrow, linear leaves, 4-6" (10-15 cm) long, shorter than the stalk when the plant blooms. Stalks: 1-6, 4-8" (10-20 cm) tall, topped by 4 or 5 sparse flowers. Flowers: bell-shaped, blue with whitish hues on the undersides of the petals.

The "Alba" cultivar has white flowers; "Spring Beauty": dark blue flowers, fragrant, long-lasting. This is the most commonly grown species.
Hardiness: Zone 2.

ANOTHER SPECIES
Scilla bifolia: native to Turkey. A solitary stalk, 3-6" (7-15 cm) tall, topped by a cluster of 1-10 flowers. Flowers: starry, blue, late-blooming. "Rosea": pink flowers, Hardiness: Zone 4. Cultivated since 1601.

TULIPA
Tulip

long with lilies, tulips are the best known decorative bulbous plants in the world.

And they come in an almost infinite range of colors and shapes. Tulips are easy to cultivate and will grow wherever they can benefit from a dormant period of a few months — downtime is essential to their life cycle.

Members of the lily family, tulips flower in the spring. All told, there are about 100 species, native to the temperate regions of Europe, the Middle East, and especially Central Asia.

Thirteenth-century origins

Tulips were flourishing long before they arrived in Europe. Indications are that the flower was already a garden fixture in the 1200s, if lines from a poem of that era can be trusted. Three hundred years later, tulips were at the heart of a flourishing trade in Turkey.

Emperor Charles V's ambassador in the Turkish city of Hadrianopolis, a Belgian named Ogier Ghiselin de Busbecq, noticed the tulips growing in local gardens. He christened them *tulipam*, a corruption of the word *tülbent*, or turban, a term frequently used in the region to identify the flower.

The ambassador dispatched a consignment of seeds and bulbs to Vienna, where they arrived in 1554. Five years later, the first flowering tulips bloomed in Europe, not only in Vienna itself, but also in the German town of Augsburg, where their presence at that time is still unexplained.

In 1561, a ship left Constantinople carrying a cargo of bulbs, that was to arrive some time later at the town of Anvers, in Flanders. From there the tulip spread throughout the rest of Europe.

Three bulbs, 30,000 florins

By 1630, there were already 140 tulip varieties on display in European gardens. The public infatuation with the flower provoked an unprecedented frenzy of speculation in the Netherlands. About 1634, "tulipomania" reached fever pitch. At a time when an annual salary was 150 florins, a single tulip fetched up to 3000 florins. In 1637, three uncommonly rare bulbs were sold for 30,000 florins, equivalent to the price of a handsome property on the banks of an Amsterdam canal. The financial crash that followed later that same year ruined thousands of speculators.

Historians even claim that tulips cost the life of the Turkish sultan, Ahmed III, whose head was chopped off in 1730. The punishment was imposed after he had been charged with overspending on an annual tulip festival.

5000 cultivars, and counting

At that period in history, more than 1300 hybrids already existed in Turkey alone.

Today, no fewer that 5600 cultivars are represented in the Classified List and International Register of Tulip Names, of which some 1250 are widely sold.

Internationaal Bloembollen Centrum

Created in 1750, the "Keizerskroon" tulip is still available for sale today.

The yellow and red tulip known as "Keizerskroon" is one of the senior members of this group. Created in 1750, it is still on sale today, more than 250 years later.

The Netherlands are still far and away the world's leading tulip-producing country with exports totalling $300 million per year, followed by France, Japan, United States, Australia, New Zealand and England. British Columbia is also a commercial player.

The most popular tulip varieties, worldwide, are "Golden Appeldoorn," "Attila," "Apeldoorn," "Queen of Night" and "Apricot Beauty." In North America, "Angélique" supplants "Attila."

A 20-year waiting period

Commercial tulip cultivation is a long, costly and complex undertaking. Hybrid growers have to start by cross-breeding two flowers in order to get the seeds and then wait for the seedlings to flower. The process takes at least five years to accomplish, sometimes twice as long.

Next, a tulip shoot will be chosen according to strict criteria. Then follows a waiting period of a few years to make certain the genetic characteristics are stable. After that, the vegetative multiplication of the bulb will begin. It will take a good 15 years to obtain 100,000 bulbs and be in a position to cater to the market on a major scale.

Bulbs are classified and sold according to their circumference. The great majority measure $4\frac{3}{4}$" (12 cm) and over, with the exception of botanical tulips, which are sometimes smaller. There are times when a tulip will produce a muta-tion. If its appearance is interesting, the new plant will be multiplied by vegetative means. The "Murillo" tulip has produced more than 80 mutations, among them the famous "Peach Blossom."

Internationaal Bloembollen Centrum

The flower itself

Tulips have only a few leaves, either basal or attached to the stalk. They are usually smooth and linear but often oval in shape. The stalk is topped by a single flower or a cluster of several flowers, at times 10-20.

Tulipa pulchella

110

Cup- or bell-shaped, the flower consists of six petals, but often twice that number. The color range is extensive, although those vivid, flamelike shades may have been caused by viruses.

Color-coordinated

Tulips need deep soil, well tilled if it is clayey, rich in peat moss or compost and very well drained. Plant the bulbs at least 6" (15 cm) deep, either in sun or partial shade.

"Golden Apeldoorn" tulip

It's a good idea to put the bulbs in the ground towards the end of September while the earth is cool, watering them thoroughly afterwards. Bulbs planted in uniform color groups always produce a better display than scattered, haphazardly colored flowers.

Place your bulbs 1½-3" (3-8 cm) apart. Some varieties with particularly lush foliage, such as those in the *kaufmanniana* and *greigii* groups, should be kept 5-6" (12-15 cm) apart as you plant them.

Watch out for squirrels!

Tulip bulbs like a dash of bonemeal in the composting material when they're planted, but this has the disadvantage of attracting squirrels and skunks. It's much better to use a fossil bone or a fertilizer designed specifically for tulips.

Some people spread a little bloodmeal on the soil to keep intruders away. Others have had some success by putting the bulbs in a paper bag with a few mothballs, then giving them a good shake before planting.

But be careful! Sensitive skins may get an allergic reaction after touching the plant. On the other hand, the bulb itself is non-toxic and was even used for nourishment in the Netherlands — as were crocus bulbs — when food was scarce during World War II.

Water sparingly

Watering and fertilizing of tulip plants can be kept to a minimum. Water the plant from time to time as it grows. Two or three moderate dressings of liquid fertilizer very low in nitrogen after the plant blooms will increase its longevity. However some gardeners recommend a single application of a balanced liquid fertilizer (10-10-10) at the moment the plants emerge from the soil.

A declaration of war

Tulips are seldom affected by disease or by garden pests. Botrytis can sometimes pose a risk, but fungicidal treatments should correct the problem if you act promptly. Aphids and garden slugs also go after the leaves, and the flowers as well, but bulb rot, caused by improper drainage, is still the major problem.

Aphids occasionally carry viruses, causing the colors of petals to become variegated, as, for exemple, with "Rembrandt" tulips. In that case, it's best to get rid of the affected bulbs and declare outright war on the aphids.

Avoiding decay

The ideal method for growing tulips is to dig them up every year after the leaves have wilted, then separate the bulbs and offsets before storing them in a cool, well-ventilated place until the fall planting season comes around.

Under normal conditions, each tulip produces two or three new bulbs that will flower the next spring. That's without counting a few small offset bulbs that should be planted in a suitable spot so they can mature further. When they are big enough to produce flowers, three to five years later, it is their turn to be placed in the flower bed.

As a general rule, however, amateur gardeners leave tulip bulbs exactly where they are until they decay and no longer produce flowers. If they are not separated each year, bulbs and offsets cluster together, begin to compete, and end up producing only meager flowers.

Sixty-year-old tulips

Certain kinds of tulip last much longer than others. With the exception of botanical tulips and the genuine species, the Darwin group takes the prize in this category.

Varieties belonging to the *kaufmanniana, greigii* and *fosteriana* groups also produce flowers year after year. "Ballade," a tulip shaped like a lily, naturalizes without difficulty and its size will increase over time. It is red, and the tips of its petals are white.

In the Montreal area I once visited a garden where tulips had been flowering faithfully for sixty years or so. They've been there so long that their varieties are no longer available on the market, and it's now virtually impossible to track down their original name. And clearly, they are not the same bulbs that flower every year.

A FEW CULTIVARS RECOMMENDED
FOR LONGEVITY

Greigii: "Candela," "Pinocchio," "Toronto," "Cape Cod," "Plaisir," "Large Copper."
Kaufmanniana: "Giuseppe Verdi," "Shakespeare," "Showwinner," "Johann Strauss," "Stresa."
Fosteriana: "Cantata," "Orange Emperor," "Juan," "Madame Lefeber," "Purissima," "Zombie."
Lily-flowered: "Aladdin," "Ballade."
Fringed: "Hamilton," "Madison Garden."
Single early: "Bellona," "Generaal de Wet," "Christmas Marvel," "Keizerskroon," "Couleur Cardinal," "Prinses's Irene."
Triumph: "Don Quichotte," "Rosario."
Darwin: "Gordon Cooper," "Oxford," "Appeldoorn," "Golden Appeldoorn," "Parade," "Pink Impression."

Renowned for its longevity, the "Pinocchio" tulip is also suitable for forcing.

Early- or late-blooming

Tulips have minimal needs, but they must be respected scrupulously.

First and foremost, well-drained soil. Next, wait until the foliage turns completely yellow before getting rid of it. If not, the bulb won't have enough time to build up reserves. The best way to camouflage the foliage is to mix tulips with other perennials in an attractive tableau or screen. It's equally important to plant them in appropriate locations, keeping their flowering periods in mind (early or late). Some flower in early May, while other varieties may still be in bloom at the end of June, especially if the weather is cool.

Internationaal Bloembollen Centrum

The "Stresa" tulip, member of the Kaufmanniana species is a very early bloomer.

114

TULIP CLASSIFICATIONS

In order to simplify the classification of tulips, botanists have established a number of categories grouping together varieties that display similar characteristics. They are:

1. Single early: cup-shaped flower, up to 3" (8 cm) across, 6-18" (15-45 cm) high. Blooms early and at mid-season. "Bellona": yellow, 10-14" (25-35 cm); "Apricot Beauty": orange-apricot, 14-16"

"Monte Carlo"

"Apricot Beauty"

(35-40 cm); "Van der Neer": mauve, 8-10" (20-25 cm).

2. Double early: double flower, cup-shaped, up to 3" (8 cm) across, 12-16" (30-40 cm) high. Blooms in mid-season. "Peach Blossom": dark pink, greenish base, 7-9" (18-23 cm); "Monte Carlo": yellow, 12-16" (30-40 cm); "Carlton": dark red, 14-16" (35-40 cm).

3. Triumph: single flower, cup-shaped, up to 2½" (6 cm) across, 14-24" (35-60 cm) high. Blooms mid-season or later. "Attila": mauve, 14-16" (35-40 cm); "Kees Nelis": red and yellow, 10-14" (25-35 cm); "Calgary": white, yellowish streaks at the tip, 8-10" (20-25 cm).

4. Darwin hybrids: single flower, egg-shaped, up to 3" (8 cm) across, 20-28" (50-70 cm) tall, various flame-like shades, edges of petals often bear-

"Beauty of Apeldoorn"

ing a contrasting color. Blooms mid-season or later. "Oxford": bright red, 20-24" (50-60 cm); "Beauty of Appeldoorn": yellow, washed with delicate orange shades, 20-24" (50-60 cm); "Pink Impression": pink, red base, 20-24" (50-60 cm).

5. Single late: cup-shaped flower, closed at the tip, up to 3" (8 cm) across, one or several stalks, color variously yellow, red, pink, white, occasionally almost black, edges of the petals often in contrasting tones, 18-30" (45-75 cm) tall. Late-blooming. "Queen of Night":

"Hamilton"

across and 18-26" (45-65 cm) tall. Late-blooming. "Queen of Sheba": burgundy red, petals edged with yellow, 22-24" (55-60 cm); "Red Shine": red, 20-24" (50-60 cm); "Elegant Lady": pale yellow, petals have reddish edges, 20-24" (50-60 cm).

7. Fringed: single cup-shaped flower, petals have delicately serrated or fringed edge, usually in a contrasting color, up to 3" (8 cm) across, 14-26" (35-65 cm) tall. Late-blooming.

"Queen of Sheba"

maroon, shading to black, 20-24" (50-60 cm); "Menton": pink with orange tones at the tips, 26-28" (65-70 cm); "Maureen": white, 26-28" (65-70 cm).

6. Lily-flowered: cup-shaped flower, single bloom, dainty, petal tips are recurved and fringed, up to 3" (8 cm)

"Queen of Night" tulips

International Bloembollen Centrum

"Spring Green"

"Fringed Elegance": yellow, 16-18" (40-45 cm); "Fringed Rhapsody": yellow, tones of red and orange, 16-18" (40-45 cm); "Crystal Beauty": dark red, 18-20" (45-50 cm).

8. Viridiflora: single cup-shaped

"Prof. Röntgen"

flower, sometimes almost closed tight, verging to green but occasionally in a different color, green tones in the center of each of the petals, up to 3" (8 cm) across, 16-22" (40-55 cm) tall. Late-blooming. "Deirdre": pink, 12-16" (30-40 cm); "Green Eyes": yellow, 18-22" (45-55 cm); "Professor Röntgen": greenish-yellow, 16-20" (40-50 cm).

9. Rembrandt: single cup-shaped flower, up to 3" (8 cm) across, variegated petals in contrasting colors caused by

"Rembrandt" tulips

a virus, 18-26" (45-65 cm) tall. Rembrandt tulips have historic associations with the age of "tulipomania" in the early seventeenth century, and are no longer available commercially. Nevertheless, for several years now, certain

118

"Estella Rijnveld"

wholesalers have begun to sell what one might call Rembrandt-brand tulips. The variegated color patterns displayed by a number of tulip varieties have become fashionable once more.

10. Parrot: single bowl-like flower with wavy petals, jagged at the edges, up to 4" (10 cm) across, 14–26" (35–65 cm) tall. Late blooming. "Blue Parrot": violet, 12–14" (30–35 cm); "Flaming Parrot": yellow, with a red streak across the center, 14–16" (35–40 cm); "Estella Rijnveld": whitish petals embellished with green, crossed by pronounced irregular bright red patches, 20–24" (50–60 cm).

The "Angélique" tulip is one of the world's most popular.

11. Double late: Bell-mouthed double flower, up to 4¾" (12 cm) across, 14-24" (35-60 cm) tall. Late-blooming. Often known as Double Peony. "Angélique": different tones of pink, 14-16" (35-40 cm); "Mount Tacoma": white, 10-16" (25-40 cm); "Uncle Tom": very dark red, 16-18" (40-45 cm).

12. Kaufmanniana: single bell-mouthed flower, upper part of the petals usually a different color from the bottom, up to 4" (10 cm) across, 6-10" (15-25 cm) tall. Leaves often

"Orange Emperor"

marked with red, purple or brown streaks. Very early blooming. Comprises the species *T. kaufmanniana* and its hybrids. "Giuseppe Verdi": red with yellow border, 12" (30 cm); "Stresa": bright red, yellow border, 10-12" (25-30 cm); "Concerto": white, 8-10" (20-25 cm).

"Red Riding Hood"

13. Fosteriana: Single bell-mouthed flower, up to 4¾" (12 cm) across, 8-26" (20-65 cm) tall, narrow leaves. Blooms in mid-season. Includes the species *T. fosteriana* and its hybrids. "Pink Emperor": pink, 12-14" (30-35 cm); "Orange Emperor": dark orange, 18-20" (45-50 cm); "White Emperor": white, 14-16" (35-40 cm).

14. Greigii: single bell-mouthed flower, up to 4" (10 cm) across, 6-12" (15-30 cm) tall. Large, outspread, pleated leaves often mottled with purple. Early blooming, sometimes at mid-season. Includes the species *T. greigii* and its hybrids. "Pinocchio": red, white border, 8-10" (20-25 cm); "Oratorio": dark

Tulipa acuminata

120

pink, 10-12" (25-30 cm); "Red Riding Hood": bright red, 10-12" (25-30 cm).

15. Other varieties: This category includes tulips that cannot be classified in the other groups, notably *T. acuminata*: single flower with long tapering petals, up to 4" (10 cm), red tips, yellow at the base, 16-18" (40-45 cm) tall. Horticultural origin.

BOTANICAL SPECIES

Botanical species that have no formal classification make up the group called "various." They include some less well-known species, even though they can be extremely attractive and long-lasting. A good many have been cultivated for a century or more.

These particular tulips will often increase in size over a period of time without special care. Normally hardy in Zone 3, most are small, producing several single flowers per stem. There are many such species, but a few stand out.

T. clusiana: solitary flowers that open out to a starry shape, up to 4" (10 cm) across, white petals mottled with red at the tips. 12" (30 cm) tall. Early to mid-season blooming. Occasionally sold as *T. chrysantha*. Native to Iran, extending to Afghanistan. Identified first in 1803.

T. kolpakowskiana: solitary wide-mouthed flower, sometimes 2-4, yellow petals marked with green on the outside, up to 3" (8 cm) across. Height: 6-8" (15-20 cm). Blooms early

Tulipa marjolettii

or at mid-season. Native to Central Asia. Zone 4. Cultivated since 1877.

T. marjoletti: solitary cup-shaped flower, cream-colored with red tones on the outside, very small, up to 1¼" (3 cm) across, 6-8" (15-20 cm) tall. Blooms early or at mid-season. Native to southern France or horticultural origin. Zone 5, probably 4. A beauty! First discovered in 1894.

T. praestans: multiple flowers, as many as 5, cup-shaped with very dark orange — almost red — petals, up to 6" (15 cm) across. 8-12" (20-30 cm)

T. praestans *"Fusilier"*

tall. Early-blooming. Native to Central Asia. First discovered in 1903. "Unicum": red, yellow base, edge of each leaf is yellowish; "Fusilier": dark orange; "Van Tubergen": red. All these cultivars are magnificent.

T. pulchella: solitary flower or in pairs (sometimes 3), cup-shaped, mauve with blackish heart, up to 3" (8 cm) across, 10-12" (25-30 cm) tall. Blooms early or at mid-season. Limited growth in Zone 4. Native to Turkey through Afghanistan. Cultivated since 1858.

T. saxatilis: as many as 4 multiple flowers, fragrant, pink shading to mauve with yellow center, up to 3" (8

cm) across, 8-10" (20-25 cm) tall. Blooms late or at mid-season. Native to Crete and Turkey. Zone 3. First discovered in 1825.

T. sylvestris: flower solitary or in pairs, pendent at budding stage, then starry, yellow, up to 3" (8 cm) across,

Tulipa turkestanica

Tulipa tarda

14-16" (35-40 cm) tall. Blooms at mid-season. Origin unknown, but naturalized from Europe to Siberia. Zone 3. Cultivated since 1753.

T. tarda: 4-15 multiple flowers, yellow at the center and tips of white petals, lightly scented, 2" (6 cm)

Tulipa urumiensis

across, flowers close at night and in dull weather. 6" (15 cm) tall. Very long-lasting. Early-blooming. Use at front of flower beds or in rock gardens. Probably the best known of all botanical tulips. Zone 3. Cultivated since 1933.

T. turkestanica: up to 12 flowers, star-shaped, occasionally giving off a disagreeable scent, white with yellow center, up to 2" (5 cm) across, 8-10"

Tulipa violacea

(20-25 cm) tall. Early or mid-season blooming. Native to Central Asia. Zone 5, probably 4. Cultivated since 1875.

T. urumiensis: flower solitary or in pairs, cup-shaped, opens widely in the sun, yellow petals often mottled with red or green on the outside, up to 3" (8 cm) across, 4-6" (10-15 cm) tall. Early-blooming. Native to Iran. Zone 5, probably 4. First discovered in 1932.

T. violacea: flower solitary or in groups of 3, star-shaped, fuschia with yellow center, up to 3" (8 cm) across, 4-10" (10-25 cm) tall. Blooms early or at mid-season. Native to Turkey, Iran and Iraq. Magnificent. Zone 4. First discovered in 1860.

OTHER SPECIES

Tulipa bakeri: native to Crete. Very like *T. saxatilis* and often considered as a member of the same species. "Lilac Wonder": pink with yellow center, 6-8" (15-20 cm). Zone 5, but probably hardier. First discovered in 1938.

Tulipa biflora: native to Turkey, star-shaped, fragrant, white with yellow center, tones of green on the outside, 4-6" (10-15 cm). Zone 5, probably 4. First discovered in 1776.

Tulipa linifolia: native to Central Asia. Red, star-shaped. Opens widely in sunlight then closes at night, 6-8" (15-20 cm). Zone 5, probably 4. First discovered in 1844.

International Bloembollen Centrum

The multiple-flowered tulip "Toronto"

Multi-flowered tulips

Multi-flowered tulips are still largely unappreciated in North America, even if several varieties have names as evocative as "Toronto," "Montreal" or "Quebec."

If they are not classified as multi-flowered wholesalers usually indicate this characteristic on the packaging under the name *Bouquet* or *Multiflowering*. They require no special attention, and some of them can grow for years without interruption, as in the case of *T. praestans* and its cultivars. Remember that a good number of botanical tulips also carry more than one flower per stalk.

Here is a short list of interesting varieties: "Claudette": white with red border; "Compostella": red with yellow border; "Montreal": yellow with an orange streak at the center of the petal; "Orange Bouquet": orange, red center; "Red Bouquet": red; "Quebec": pink, yellow border; "Sylvia Warder": pink, yellow border; "Toronto": red. The "Quebec" tulip is a mutation of "Toronto."

The "Angélique" mystery

Some tulips, however, can produce multiple flowers after special heat treatment. I remember a springtime when the "Angéliques" I had planted the previous autumn all produced stalks bearing two, three or even five huge flowers. A superb display! This magnificent late-blooming double tulip is pink and white.

The secret of this floral phenomenon was due to faulty storage conditions. "Ad Rem," "Abba," "Angélique," "Monsella," "Monte Carlo," "Kees Nelis" and "Viking" all reacted in this way when the bulbs were exposed to a constant temperature of 73°F (23°C) for two to four weeks. But the tulips returned to normal later on.

Robert Nadon, *La Presse*

"Angélique" tulips at the author's home.

A pleasant scent

If tulips are renowned above all for the sheer beauty of their flowers, a few beguile us with their fragrance.

The following cultivars belong in this group: "Ad Rem": red and orange; "Allegretto": red, yellow border; "Angelique": white with pink tones; "Apricot Parrot": pink with gree streaks; "Bellona": yellow; "Ballerina": orange "Christmas Marvel": pale pink; "Cardinal": dark red with violet tones; "Daydream": yellow; "Golden Melody": yellow; "Monte Carlo": yellow; "Orange Sun": bright orange; "Princess Irene": orange with broad violet streaks.

Forcing

It is not difficult to force tulips in order to get pretty potted flowers during the winter and early spring.

Put the bulbs side by side (without touching each other) in a 6" (15 cm-wide) pot filled with regular potting soil, the "nose" of the bulb just below the

surface of the soil. Put the pot in the refrigerator or a cold room, between 35 and 50°F (2 and 10°C) for a 15–16-week period, either in darkness or semi-darkness.

When the stems reach a height of 2-4" (5-10 cm), put them in a cool, well-lit spot, near a window, for example, but away from direct sunlight. If the room is cool enough, flowering will last about a week, sometimes longer. But if the air is too warm, as is often the case in our apartments, the flowers will quickly fade.

Blooms in the garden

If you want to reuse the bulbs in the garden, cut the wilted flower and fertilize the plant with a balanced food or one low in nitrogen, until the foliage dies.

You should then stop watering and dig up the new bulbs when the soil is dry. You can plant them in the garden in the fall. Under normal conditions, they will flower the following spring.

Another forcing method is to leave the bulbs just as they are, in the fridge or a cold room, always at a temperature between 35 and 50°F (2 and 10°C), for the normal period of time. After planting, leave the pot at room temperature, but not too warm. The flowers will appear two or three weeks later.

In this particular case, if you take care of the seedlings until the leaves die, the new bulbs planted the next fall will generally take two years to bloom.

Opposite page: "Ad Rem" tulip

"Quebec" tulip

Indigenous Plants

Arisaema
Erythronium
Lilium canadense
Polygonatum
Sanguinaria
Trillium

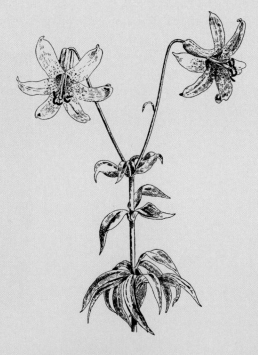

$\mathcal{T}$he Jack-in-the-pulpit rises up majestically in its spathe, a large leaf shaped like a church pulpit. Hence, its name.

Elegant in appearance, it displays a rigid stem set off by a multitude of tiny flowers — the spadix. The Jack-in-the-pulpit emerges from a cylinder formed by a leaf whose particular shape is the result of a long evolutionary process. This is the spathe.

In some plants, the spathe assumes the shape of a hood that overhangs the spadix, sometimes hiding it from view. During the summer the foliage falls off, baring the main stem, which is by then covered with a small cluster of bright red berries.

There are more than 150 species of *arisaema* native to virtually every corner of the globe — in northeastern North America, eastern and central Africa, as well as the temperate and tropical regions of Asia.

A natural wonder

Among certain species, the spathe is almost a work of art. The most commonly found species in eastern North America is the *A. triphyllum*, which sports a greenish or whitish spathe, striped with symmetrical white streaks.

Arisaemas usually have two or three large upright leaves, each consisting of three leaflets carried on a stem up to 16" (40 cm) tall.

Jardin botanique de Montréal

Arisaema triphyllum

A word of caution

These plants grow in a moist soil, well drained and rich in organic matter. They usually require dappled shade, but at my place, they've thrived for years in a corner of the garden with a northern exposure where the sun never penetrates.

Arisaema tubers are usually sold by catalogue in the spring. They should be planted 4-8" (10-20 cm) deep. You can also find *A. triphyllum* seedlings at a few nurseries in the indigenous plant section. Normally, they take their time before showing up in the spring.

Multiplication is brought about by dividing the rhizome or the tuber. The latex exuded by the bulb is an irritant and may cause severe burning if it comes in contact with the mouth.

If you are patient enough, seedlings can be used to grow the plants. But the seeds themselves will need one or two cold spells to germinate, and there is at least a five-year wait before the first bloom appears. Arisaemas are occasionally susceptible to mildew, and slugs enjoy a chance to put them on their menu.

ARISAEMA AMURENSE

Origin: northern regions of Russia and China.

Flowering period: June.

Description: usually a solitary leaf, 5 leaflets 4-6" (10-15 cm) long. Greenish spadix, spathe greenish or purple, striped with white or yellow. Overall height: up to 18" (45 cm).

Hardiness: Zone 5, probably 4.

ARISAEMA SIKOKIANUM

Origin: Japan.

Flowering period: June.

Description: two leaves, with 3 to 5 leaflets, 2-6" (5-15 cm) long. White spadix, purple spathe, but white on the inside. The upper part is striped with pink and the spadix is free standing. Overall height: up to 20" (50 cm).

Hardiness: Zone 5.

ARISAEMA TRIPHYLLUM

Dark red arisaema, Jack-in-the-pulpit

Origin: eastern North America.

Flowering period: June.

Description: two leaves, with three leaflets, 3-6" (8-15 cm) long. The spadix is purple; the spathe is greenish, sometimes purple, occasionally has a whitish base flushed with purple. Overall height: 24-36" (60-90 cm). Seeds need to be treated for several weeks in order to germinate. At times classified as *A. atrorubens*.

Hardiness: Zone 3.

Jardin botanique de Montréal

Arisaema triphyllum

Dog's-Tooth Violet

Erythroniums are among the first flowers to peep out from the under-growth in early May.

They cover the ground of our maple woods with a crowd of little yellow hanging bells, petals curved backward, their purple — sometimes yellow — anthers in plain view. And you will find similar colonies in a wide range of habitats.

Easy to grow, erythroniums are bulbous plants that are still relative strangers to many gardens even though several varieties and cultivars are commercially available. They are all entrancing, thought by many to be the loveliest of all spring wildflowers.

A canine tooth

There are 20 species of erythronium, all native to the temperate zones of North America, the exceptions being *E. dens-canis*, which comes from Europe and Asia, and *E. japonicum*, native to Japan. They are members of the lily family.

The name comes from the Greek word *erythros*, meaning red, an allusion to the color of *E. dens-canis*, even if the real color tends to pink rather than red. The bulb's shape is not unlike a dog's tooth, hence the Latin name *Erythronium dens-canis*. The plant is also known as Trout Lily, after the pretty speckles found on the leaves of some species.

The majority of commercially sold erythroniums are frost-hardy and form attractive clumps. Some adapt well to naturalization. The smallest species, *E. dens-canis*, can be planted in a lawn.

Erythronium dens-canis

Avoid dehydration

Erythroniums like humus-rich soil, moist and well-drained, in partial shade — beneath a large tree, for example. Leaves and stems usually disappear in late May or early June, later for some cultivars.

Plant bulbs 4-6" (10-15 cm) deep, in early fall, because they are inclined to dehydrate — and that is something to keep an eye on when you buy them. Discard any bulbs showing signs of dryness.

Erythroniums multiply by producing offsets. You may also use seed, but that involves a five-year process, as is so often the case with seeds and seedlings. Some species, in particular *E. americanum*, our native erythronium, produce many offsets before the first flower appears.

Retractile roots

It was the Quebec botanist Brother Marie-Victorin who first described this plant in detail in his monumental study, *Flore Laurentienne* (Flora of the Laurentians). The new shoot is protected by a hard tip, permitting it to break through the soil, pierce the carpet of dead leaves, and even move out of the way small objects that prevent it from reaching sunlight. And this tiny awl-like tool stays in place at the tip of one of the leaves.

The plant has retractile roots, which allow the bulb to settle down gradually to its ideal depth — a common feature of bulbous plants.

Erythroniums are not disease- or insect-prone, but our old friends the slugs won't pass them up, when given the opportunity.

Commercial production is largely concentrated in the Netherlands.

Erythronium *"White Beauty"*

ERYTHRONIUM AMERICANUM

North American Erythronium

Origin: northeastern North America, west to Minnesota, southward to Florida.

Description: pale green, lance-shaped horizontal leaves, 4-6" (10-15 cm) long, mottled with white and brown. Stalk: 6-12" (15-30 cm). Flower: solitary, 1½-2" (3-5 cm) long. Color: yellow, pink tones on the outside.

Flowering period: early May.

Cultivation: easy to grow in shady position, but several specimen are sterile, non-flowering, with a single leaf. The young stocks take a few years to flower.

Hardiness: Zone 3.

ERYTHRONIUM DENS-CANIS

Dog's-tooth violet

Origin: Europe, Asia.

Description: lance-shaped, heavily mottled leaves in tones of dark brown laced with pink, 4-6" (10-15 cm) long. Stalk: 6" (15 cm), sometimes twice that. Flower: solitary, 1½-2" (3-5 cm) long. Color: pink.

Flowering period: early May.

Cultivation: easy. Very robust. Several cultivars of *E. album* are available: "Album" and "Snowflake," white; "White Splendor": white with brownish center; "Frans Hals": dark pink; "Rose Queen": pink.

Hardiness: Zone 4, probably 3.

ERYTHRONIUM REVOLUTUM

Origin: southern British Columbia (Vancouver Island), California.

Flowering period: Mid-May.

Description: lance-shaped leaves, 6-8" (15-20 cm) long, dark green mottled with dark brown, cultivars much paler. Color: dark pink.

Cultivation: easy. The "Pagoda" cultivar, a cross between *E. revolutum* and *E. tuolumnense*, is very popular. Stalk: 12-16" (30-40 cm). Flower: yellow, brown center, from 2-5, sometimes as many as 10. Very pretty and robust. "White Beauty" cultivar: Stalk: 6" (15 cm); white or very pale yellow flowers; robust. It is also regarded as a cultivar of *E. californicum*. "Pink Beauty": bright pink.

Hardiness: Zone 4.

Internationaal Bloembollen Centrum

Erythronium revolutum *"Pagoda"*

$\mathcal{L}$ILIUM CANADENSE

Canada Lily

$\mathcal{T}$he Canada lily is one of the loveliest of North America's native flowers and deserves a special place in anyone's garden.

Its yellow and orange petals, often flecked with brown, its flowers perched atop a stalk easily 5' (1.5 m) tall and more, inevitably catch the eye, all the more so since the plant will often bloom for three weeks.

On occasion, the flowers are dark orange — if not bright red — a coloring that may be attributable to a virus but does not appear to affect the plant. There is also a rare wild variety of the lily called either *rubrum* or *coccineum*, which has red flowers.

Together with *L. bulbiferum* and *L. trigrinum*, which the early colonists brought to North America from Europe and have since naturalized in some areas, the Philadelphia lily (*L. philadelphicum*) and the Canada lily are the only lilies to have become part of our native flora.

Available from nurseries

For a number of years, *Lilium canadense* has been available from nurseries specializing in indigenous plants, where they are reproduced from seed or by dividing the bulbs. Some cultivars have also been developed, but they are hard to find.

In their natural element, Canada lilies grows in wet locations, that are often flooded in the spring. They can be found in sunny conditions, as well as in the shade of the woods. They are hardy in Zone 3.

The stem rises from a scale-covered bulb that is solidly attached to a rhizome. Every year, the rhizome produces a new bulb, the parent bulb having disappeared during its annual growth cycle.

From 3-6" (7-15 cm) long, the lance-shaped and clearly denticulated leaves are arranged in circular fashion around the stem, each group evenly distanced from the next. The flowers are located at the top of the stem, at the tip of a peduncle that may sometimes be 6" (15 cm) long. Bell-shaped, they are curved backward and pendent.

Beware the lily beetle!

Canada lilies prefer a slightly acid soil, deep, rich in organic matter and able to retain moisture, in a partly shady location. They will also grow in relatively heavy soil. If the environment isn't wet enough in the spring and up to the time of flowering, the Canada lily tends to degenerate, the stems growing smaller and bearing fewer flowers.

Canada lilies start flowering at the end of June and when they are mature, produce large fruit, which dry easily. The stems then make magnificent bouquets.

These lilies seem barely affected by disease, but the crioceris or lily beetle is a formidable foe. Unless you intervene in good time, the leaves and even the flowers risk disappearing within a few days once the little red insect has invaded the plant. Use an appropiate pesticide or pick the insects off by hand.

Pierre McCann, *La Presse*

Some Canada lilies produce deep orange, almost red, flowers.

136

℘OLYGONATUM

Solomon's Seal

ℰ legantly stylish, with arching stem, alternate leaves and pendent, yellowish, small bell-like flowers, Solomon's Seal is a distinctive garden
plant.

If they fertilize themselves, which is not always the case, the flowers will
turn into pretty — but slightly toxic — small red or very dark blue berries.

Some 30 species are native to North America, Europe and Asia. The plant
belongs to the lily family.

Identified 2000 years ago

P. pubescens, a variety of Solomon's Seal bearing blackish fruit, is frequently sold
by nurseries in the indigenous plant department.

However, the most widely sold species at first-class garden centers are *P.
multiflorum*, as well as the splendid *P. odoratum* "Variegatum," with delicately
pale yellow variegated leaves and red stems when the plant is young. Hardy in
Zone 3, both are native to Europe and Asia.

Polygonatum pubescens, *or the indigenous Solomon's Seal*

The Greek term *polygonatum* means "many angles" or "joints." The word was first used in the context of flowers around 2000 years ago by Pedanius Dioscorides, a Greek military surgeon and botanist.

The name Solomon's Seal refers to the scar left each year on the rhizome after the stem disappears. Legend has it that King Solomon stamped the rhizome with his own seal in recognition of its medicinal value, a story perhaps based more on imagination than reality.

Happy in the shade

Solomon's Seal likes a soil rich in humus, well drained yet able to retain moisture. It grows well in full or partial shade.

Polygonatum needs no special fertilizer but is almost impossible to transplant. It's also advisable to leave the rhizomes where they are for some time so that handsome beds can be established.

Propagate by dividing the rhizomes or the clumps. Seedlings offer only half-hearted results, especially since germination can be a slow process and because the offspring do not always correspond to the parents. Moreover, the seeds must be kept in cold storage for several weeks before they will germinate.

Solomon's Seal is virtually disease-free, but slugs and bugs may alter the foliage.

$\mathcal{S}$ANGUINARIA

Bloodroot

$\mathcal{S}$anguinaria belong to the poppy family, although there is just one species in the world and it is found in eastern North America. Its name derives from its root, which exudes a blood-red substance when it is broken.

Sanguinaria are not considered bulbous plants; their roots are more like rhizomes. You can find them in the fall at specialist bulb emporiums.

There is a cultivar with multiple flowers that comes from the Netherlands, though the plant is often cultivated elsewhere in Europe. Look for sanguinaria in nurseries among native perennials.

Ornamental leaves

The plant's flowering is short-lived, as the petals — between 8 and 16 — drop off within a few days. It is a brief, but nevertheless magnificent, showing. The leaves are rolled together aorund the stalk and open gently during or at the end of blooming, one by one. Large, kidney-shaped, lobed and very ornamental, they stay green for most of the summer.

Sanguinaria will multiply by seed or by division of the rhizomes after the leaves have wilted. Sanguinaria is untroubled by disease or insects.

Pierre McCann, *La Presse*

Sanguinaria is a magnificent native plant, but its flowers are short-lived.

SANGUINARIA CANADENSIS

Origin: eastern North America.
Flowering period: early May.
Description: leaves 6-12" (15-30 cm) long. Stalk: 12" (30 cm). Flowers: solitary, ³/₄-1¹/₂" (2-4 cm) across, horizontal, close up in the evening.
Color: White, at times pinkish, yellow center.
Cultivation: deep soil, cool, fairly rich in nutrients, moist, well-drained, shady location. Plant adapts well in shady rock gardens, wildflower gardens, or under trees.

The "Multiplex" cultivar has two flowers and blooms for longer than *S. canadensis*. If its flower is bigger, its height on the other hand is smaller. The stalk is barely 8" (20 cm) tall. It is often sold under the name of the "Flore Pleno" or "Plena" cultivar. We are talking about a very special flower — unfortunately, the rhizome is expensive. But as it fairly rapidly forms little tufts, you can give one to your friends.
Hardiness: Zone 4, possibly 3. "Multiplex" is a little more fragile.

Jardin botanique de Montréal

Sanguinaria's "Multiplex" cultivar produces a lovely double flower.

$\mathcal{T}$RILLIUM

Trillum, Wake Robin

$\mathcal{I}$n the northeastern regions of Canada and the United States, there is no more familiar spring wildflower than the trillium.

They create large colonies of white (*T. grandiflorum*) or spectacularly large wine-red flowers (*T. erectum*), although the latter spread farther apart. In addition, there is a daintier white flower marked in its center by a dark pink or red triangle (*T. undulatum*).

Some indigenous varieties have long been available commercially, but there are a number of less well known varieties, some in their original state, that also deserve a place in the garden.

The name trillium refers to the figure three, corresponding to the number of leaves and petals on the flower. Trilliums grow from rhizomes and there are about 30 species native to North America, as well as northeastern Asia and the Himalayas. They all shed their leaves during the summer.

Jardin botanique de Montréal

The white trillium — Trillium grandiflorum — is a familiar variety.

Mottled leaves

There is a single stalk, and the flower is solitary. The green sepals are clearly visible at the corner of each petal. Gathered at the head of the stalk, the leaves are sessile (attached directly to the base), lanceolate, often oval or elliptical. Some leaves are heavily mottled.

Native trilliums grow in maple groves, but *T. undulatum*, or wavy trillium, needs a more acid soil and is therefore found amongst conifers, away from our gardens.

Trilliums do best in rich soil, augmented with compost every year, in partial shade or beneath leafy trees, provided that the root carpet is not too thick, as it can be, for example, in maple forests. The flowers like a moist but well-drained environment. Plant the fleshy rhizome 4-6" (10-15 cm) deep.

The plant will increase in size with time, but it can also be propagated by gently dividing the root during the summer, after the leaves have gone. Seed can be used as well; however, be prepared to wait five years for the first flowers.

Disease is not a problem, but snails and slugs enjoy the leaves of young trilliums.

Commercial production, either from seed or by rhizome separation, is still carried out on a small scale. It is concentrated in western Canada and the United States. Some varieties are easier to find in catalogues than in nurseries.

TRILLIUM CERNUUM

Hanging trillium

Origin: eastern North America.
Description: leaves 2-6" (5-15 cm). Spike (stalk): dainty, 8-10" (20-25 cm). Peduncle: ½-1½" (1-4 cm). Flower: pendulous, 1½" (4 cm) in diameter. Color: pinkish, sometimes white; purple ovary and anthers.
Flowering period: May.
Cultivation: a cool spot, moist or wet. Indigenous and frost-hardy.
Hardiness: Zone 3.

TRILLIUM ERECTUM

Red trillium

Origin: eastern North America.
Flowering period: May.
Description: leaves up to 12" (30 cm) long. Stalk: robust, 8-16" (20-40 cm). Peduncle: 1-4" (2-10 cm). Flower: dark red; yellow anthers.
Cultivation: very easy. *T. erectum album* variety; white flowers, sometimes flushed with pink; yellow anthers. *T. erectum luteum* variety: greenish.
Hardiness: Zone 3. White-flowered varieties may be more fragile.

TRILLIUM GRANDIFLORUM

White trillium

Origin: eastern North America.
Flowering period: May.
Description: leaves up to 12" (30 cm) long. Stalk: robust 8-18" (20-45 cm). Peduncle: 1½-3" (4-8 cm). Flowers: 3-7" (8-14 cm) across. Color: white, shading to a soft pink before wilting; yellow anthers.

Jardin botanique de Montréal

The petals of Trillium grandiflorum *become pink as they mature.*

Cultivation: easy in a moist and humus-rich soil. "Florepleno" variety: double flower, white; "Roseum": double flower, pink. Hard to find.
Hardiness: Zone 3.

Trillium luteum

Pierre McCann, La Presse

TRILLIUM LUTEUM
Yellow trillium
Origin: southeastern United States.
Flowering period: May.
Description: green leaves, 6" (15 cm) long, mottled with paler green. Stalk: up to 18" (45 cm). Flower: sessile and upright. Color: yellow, sometimes tinged with green. Handsome and unusual.
Cultivation: easy.
Hardiness: Zone 5, probably 4.

TRILLIUM SESSILE
Sessile trillium
Origin: northeastern United States.
Flowering period: May.
Description: leaves 5-6" (12-15 cm) long, mottled in pale green or maroon. Stalk: up to 12" (30 cm). Flower: sessile, upright. Color: purple (sepals and petals). Magnificent specimen.
Cultivation: easy. "Snow Queen" cultivar: white; "Rubrum": purple. Both hard to find.
Hardiness: Zone 5, probably 4.

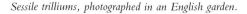

Sessile trilliums, photographed in an English garden.

International Bloembollen Centrum

Agapanthus
Anemone
Arum
Babiana
Begonia
Bletilla
Caladium
Canna
Cardiocrinum
Colocasia
Crocosmia
Dahlia
Eucomis
Freesia
Galtonia
Gladiolus
Gloriosa
Homeria
Hymenocallis
Ixia
Leucocoryne
Lilium
Nerine
Ornithogalum
Polianthes
Ranunculus
Sparaxis
Tigridia
Triteleia
Zantedeschia
Zephyranthes

Summer

AGAPANTHUS

Agapanthus

The Agapanthus has an unusually long stem crowned by an umbel of tubular flowers, usually blue, but sometimes violet or white. There are a dozen or so species, all native to South Africa, as well as a good number of cultivars. The plant's name combines the Greek words for "flower" and "love."

It produces excellent cut flowers, which make it a favorite among florists. In the garden, they normally bloom in July. At maturity, the stalk is covered by very attractive small fruit. The Headbourne hybrids, which are the hardiest, can withstand winter conditions in Zone 5 with the help of a thick mulch. Others are used as summer bulbs.

Agapanthus prefer fertile soil, capable of retaining moisture, and a sunny location. Plant the bulbs 2-3" (5-8 cm) deep. Watering should be reduced once the flowers have stopped blooming. They will also thrive as potted plants, as long as they are fertilized regularly. In this case use the largest bulbs to ensure the best-looking blooms.

Agapanthus increase their numbers by root division. Seedlings may be used for fertile hybrids. Slugs occasionally take a liking to the leaves, and during a heat wave the plant is susceptible to spider mites and thrips.

AGAPANTHUS AFRICANUS

Agapanthe

Origin: South Africa.

Flowering period: July.

Description: lanceolate, narrow leaves, 4–14" (10–35 cm) long. Stalk: 24–36" (60–90 cm). Flowers: $^3/_4$–2" (2–5 cm) long, umbel: 4–6" (10–15 cm) in diameter.

Color: dark blue

Cultivation: easy. *A. africanus* "Albus": white. Other cultivars unidentified: "Blue Triumphator": bright blue; "Blue Giant": blue; Headbourne hybrids: "Pinocchio": dark blue, small.

Agapanthus do well as potted plants.

Internationaal Bloembollen Centrum

ANEMONE
Windflower

The anemones are a group of about 120 species of herbaceous, rhizomatous or tuberous plants that appear in a variety of forms. Some are enormously popular both in our gardens and at the flower shop.

The name derives from the Greek word *anemos*, meaning "wind," and in the ancient world it was believed that the wind made anemones flower. Their foliage is similar to the plants of the *ranunculus* family, to which anemones belong.

Several varieties, such as the Canada anemone, the Japanese anemones (*A. hupehensis*) and their numerous hybrids, are considered to be rhizomatous perennials, although the tuberous species such as the florists' anemone (*A. coronaria*), are generally classified among bulbous plants.

You can buy the small dry tubers for growing tuberous anemones at the same time as other spring and summer bulbs.

A ruff of leaves

Most anemones produce round or oval-shaped basal leaves, although the leaves attached to the stalk are usually denticulated, sometimes without a peduncle, and arranged like a ruff beneath the flower, as in the case of *A coronaria*.

Anemones thrive best in a moist, humus- or compost-rich soil, well-drained, either in partial shade or sunlight, but set in a cool place and sheltered from the midday sun. The soil should be acid-free preferably without peat moss. Some varieties, like *A. blanda* and *A. ranunculoides,* proliferate and form colonies, if grown under the right conditions. Their leaves will drop off in summer when it is hot and dry just before the plant grows dormant.

Plant the tubers at least 4" (10 cm) deep, after soaking them in water for a whole day. The dried tubers, which look like little claws, contain barely 15 percent water and can be kept for two or three years.

Plant it on its side

It is often hard to decide exactly how to put the tuber in the ground, but occasionally you can find a little circle on the tuber's surface, from which the plant grows. If you can't find this, plant the tuber on its side.

Commercial producers use seed to multiply *A. blanda* and *A. coronaria*. It's also possible to separate the tubers while the plant is dormant. But the tubers can be damaged in the process, causing a fatal disease.

Anemones are vulnerable to a number of diseases, especially oidium, mildew and leaf fungus. Slugs, aphids and caterpillars are among the garden pests that the anemone attracts.

Extremely popular with florists, anemones are produced mainly in the Netherlands, France, England, Israel and the United States.

Anemone blanda *"Blue shade"*

Internationaal Bloembollen Centrum

ANEMONE BLANDA

Greek anemone

Origin: southeastern Europe, Turkey, extending to the Caucasus.

Flowering period: May.

Description: no basal leaf. Leaves on the stalk are short-lived, heavily serrated, 2 or 3 in number, irregularly divided in 3 segments. Stalk: about 4" (10 cm). Flower: very large in relation to the height of the stalk, ¾-1½" (2-4 cm) in diameter with 10-15 petals. Color: blue, mauve, white or red. They close at night.

Cultivation: easy. Dazzling flowers grow in large numbers. A mulch will protect the bulbs during winter. Cultivars are numerous: "Blue Star": pale blue with a yellow center;

"Charmer": pink; "Radar": dark pink; "White Splendor": large white flowers and a pinkish exterior. Often sold as a mixture of colors.

Hardiness: Zone 5.

ANEMONE CORONARIA

Poppy anemone

Origin: Mediterranean basin.

Flowering period: generally speaking, *A. coronaria* is considered a spring-flowering plant. However, since our northern summers are very warm, the temperate weather needed to help the flowers bloom in the spring is usually far too short to permit several flowers to appear. During the summer the foliage tends to fade and disappear, a sign that the bulb is becoming dormant. On the other hand, blooming — at times abundant — will often occur in September, lasting until the first frost.

Description: basal leaves divided in 3. The leaves on the stalk are sessile, noticeably serrated. Stalk: 6-8" (15-20 cm) high, sometimes 12" (30 cm). Flowers: solitary, from 5 to 8 petals, 1¼-2¼" (3-6 cm) in diameter. Colors: a wide range.

Cultivation: compost-rich soil, moist, well-drained, preferably in a location of dappled shade. It is advisable to plant tubers every three years. There are many cultivars. The De Caen varieties produce single flowers with 5 to 8 petals, resembling the

Anemone blanda

152

Anemone coronaria *"De Caen"*

Pierre McCann, *La Presse*

poppy. The different shades are vibrant, and come in blue, violet, pink, red, etc. Often sold as a mix. The St. Brigid types produce double flowers, often in pastel or two-color tones. Some cultivars produce white flowers. This anemone has been grown since 1870.

Hardiness: Zone 5, with winter protection.

ANEMONE RANUNCULOIDES
Origin: Europe and northern Italy.
Flowering period: May.
Description: often lacks basal leaves. Leaves on the stalk often towards the tip of the stem, very dark green, serrated. Stalk: up to 6" (15 cm). Flowers: 4-5 petals, from ³/₄-1¹/₄" (2-3 cm) in diameter. Color: bright yellow.
Cultivation: well-drained moist soil, shady location, under the trees. Tolerates dry soil during the summer.

In his *Flore laurentienne*, botanist Brother Marie-Victorin reported that the anemone was naturalized in Saint-Jean-sur-Richelieu and its vicinity. Quickly forms clumps. Sold by catalogue.
Hardiness: Zone 4.

Another variety
Anemone nemorosa: wood anemone. Ferny leaves. Stalk: 4" (10 cm). Solitary flower, ³/₄-1¹/₄" (2 to 3 cm) in diameter. Color: white on the outside with tones of purple or pink. Flowers in May. There are many cultivars.

Anemone nemorosa *"Wood anemone"*

Jardin botanique de Montréal

153

$\mathcal{A}$RUM

Cuckoo Pints, Lord-and-Ladies

$\mathcal{T}$he Arum group includes the gigantic *Amorphophallus titanum*, an extraordinary plant that produces the largest flower in existence. It blooms only sporadically, but it usually makes the international headlines whenever a botanical garden advertises this rare display.

The cowl-like spathe can measure up to 60" (1.5 m) in diameter and 10' (3 m) in circumference. The erect spadix extends as high as 80" (2 m). This huge flower also has the distinction of being one of the most foul-smelling in the world. It is sometimes raised on a peduncle 40" (1 m) tall and its root — a corm — measures up to 60" (1.5 m) in diameter, and weighs as much as 110 lbs (50 kilos). Needless to say, this tropical species does not grow here in North America.

Arums are members of the huge *aracene* family, which includes the Jack-in-the-pulpit, *zantedeschias*, and the splendid calla lily.

The arum's spectacular flower is formed by a colorful spathe — in effect a leaf modified by centuries of evolution — and by the spadix — the plant's reproductive organ — which protrudes from the center of the spathe.

Beautiful berries

Arums of less formidable dimensions number some 26 varieties of tuberous plants with arrow-shaped leaves. Their scientific name derives from the Greek word *aron*, meaning "wheat," and the plants come from the warm or semi-tropical regions of southern Europe, North Africa and Asia Minor. The species grown in North America during the summer is *Arum italicum*, a native of North Africa and Europe, from southern England as far as Turkey.

Internationaal Bloembollen Centrum

Arum italicum

154

A. italicum has arrow-shaped, often reticulated leaves, 6-12" (15-30 cm) long, green, at times splashed with yellow, and extremely ornamental. The greenish-white spathe — from 6 to 16" (15-40 cm) high — appears in the summer, usually in July, and produces a compact, long-lasting cluster of pretty red berries, for which it is highly prized.

Water gardens

Plant the tuber 3-4" (8-10 cm) deep in well-drained, rich soil. The earth should be moist during the growing period, drier when the plant is dormant, in partial shade and protected from the wind. The plant does well near ponds and water gardens, where it benefits from the humid atmosphere. Water regularly while the plant is growing. Feed once a month with a balanced ferilizer.

Store tubers in a cool place during the winter. Potted plants need less water during the winter after the leaves have wilted.

Propagate by dividing the clumps and transplanting the bulblets removed while the plant is dormant, or even by seeding. If you use seed, you will have to remove the seeds from their fleshy sheath, a procedure that may irritate the skin.

Arums are relatively free from disease or insect damage.

Amorphophallus titanum, *photographed in a botanical garden on the island of Java, in Indonesia. The spadix is 55" (140 cm) high and the spathe measures 37¹/₂"(95 cm) in diameter. The plant blooms every four years.*

Reuter

$\mathcal{B}$ABIANA

Babiana

$\mathcal{B}$abianas are corm-grown and are usually cultivated in pots, but they also do well in gardens.

Reaching a height of 12" (30 cm), the stalk — often divided — carries flowers ¾–1½" (2 to 4 cm) in diameter, in spikes. The flowers have six petals, with a darker color at the center, and are fragrant. Blooming occurs in June. Leaves are lanceolate but often fan-shaped, numbering seven or eight.

Native to South Africa, babiana is a Latinized version of the Afrikaans word for baboon (*babiaan*), and is also known in English as Baboon Flower. Baboons like to eat the bulbs.

The Kew Hybrids

Babianas belong to the iris family and there are about 60 species. They are often sold under the name of their cultivars, such as "Kew Hybrids," and their colors are extremely varied.

The bulbs should be planted 4" (10 cm) deep in light, well-drained, compost-rich soil, in a warm, sunny or partly shady location. They need to be kept in a cool place when the leaves have faded, an appropriate time to divide the numerous bulblets.

Babianas make excellent potted plants. They need sunshine or bright light. Feed the plants with a light, balanced fertilizer for three full weeks before they flower. Watering stops when the leaves turn yellow. The plant is occasionally bothered by spider mites.

Horticolor

Babiana *"Kew Hybrids"*

BEGONIA

Begonia

or more than 100 years begonias have captivated garden lovers. For that reason the plants are the subject of intense research by hybrid developers. Each year new varieties come on the market, to the extent that today thousands of hybrids are for sale.

It is in fact a global industry, with headquarters located in Belgium, United States, Germany and England. Tens of millions of tubers are sold each year worldwide.

Begonias make up a large family in their own right. There are nearly 1000 species, originating from almost every corner of the globe, but especially the Americas. Modern varieties are descended from South American species. In 1690 the flower was named in honor of Michel Bégon, a French patron of science who was governor of the Caribbean island of Santo Domingo at the time.

Tuberous begonia

Flowers that last for years

The tuber of the tuberous begonia hydrid looks rather like a thick disk, with a slight depression in the center of one of its sides. Unlike many other bulbous plants, it does not produce bulblets. Instead, the tuber grows bigger every year. The plant can be propagated in the garden by dividing the tuber into sections.

If grown in appropriate conditions and properly stored during the winter, the tubers will continue to produce flowers for years. Some writers even say 30 or 40 years. However, a 2- to 14-year span is considered normal. After 10 years, the tuber can reach an astonishing diameter of 12" (30 cm).

Male flowers are bigger

The begonias sold today are horticulturally produced and are grouped together under the scientific name *Begonia x tuberhybrida*. They are subdivided into a number of categories according to their shape, height, flower structure or their floral sheath (perianth).

Jacques Allard

Tuberous begonia

The leaves of tuberous hybrids are alternate, single, often veined, sometimes lanceolate or heart-shaped depending on their group, covered in fine hairs, and up to 8" (20 cm) long on occasion.

The flowers themselves, made up of quite distinct petals and sepals, are unisexual. The larger flowers, the males, are found at the central tip of the stalk, while the smaller, female, flowers are arranged on both sides.

Tuberous begonias are grown either by planting the tubers or transplanting seedlings produced in greenhouses, at the end of December or the beginning of January. Such is the case with the so-called "Non-Stop" double-flowered begonias that generally bloom until the first frost.

Tubers or seeds?

Seedling begonias may be less expensive than tubers, but their quality is commensurate with the price. They are smaller, more often affected by disease, and their flowers are less showy. And at the end of the season, the tuber cannot be re-used because it hasn't had time to store up reserves, all its energy having been devoted to producing flowers.

In commercial production, the flowers are cut so as to allow the tuber to increase in size, as is the case with tulips and the majority of other flowering bulbs. For this reason each tuber costs several dollars.

Tubers planted in the garden will produce seedlings that are sometimes 24" (60 cm) wide and an equivalent height; in fact, it is sometimes necessary to stake them up in order to protect them from the wind. As for the flowers, they can reach 3-6" (8-15 cm) in diameter.

Don't get the leaves wet

Begonias like a rich, well-drained, slightly acidic soil, bolstered with compost and peat moss to help retain moisture. They are happiest in partial shade or exposed to morning sun, in an open area.

Water the plants regularly, taking care not to wet the leaves. In hot, humid weather, the plant is susceptible to botrytis, oidium and rotting of the neck.

It's a good idea to fertilize begonias every 15 days, alternating between a balanced ingredient (20-20-20) and a formula 15-30-15.

After the first serious frost, dig up the tubers and let them dry in the open air for about 15 days. Then wipe off the remaining traces of earth and store the tubers in vermiculite or peat moss at a temperature between 40° and 45°F (5° and 7°C). It is also a good idea to dust them with a fungicide to reduce the risk of rot during storage.

Plant them indoors

Divide the plants every two or three years. Cut the tuber in two sections and powder the incision with a fungicide. Then allow the tubers to dry for a few days before transplanting them.

It's better to plant tubers indoors before moving them to the garden at the end of May.

To grow the plants in containers, just plant a bulb in a pot 8" (20 cm) in diameter, only half-full of soil. Place the lower side of the tuber towards the top and cover lightly with potting soil. Keep only the tuber's strongest stem, removing all the others. As the plant grows larger, add more earth.

Stop watering in the fall and store the pot in a cool, dimly lit spot.

Begonias can be multiplied by taking cuttings. Growing from seed is a long and exacting business, but it can be done in the house. However, the plants produced in this way do not always match up to the effort expended.

Begonia "Golden Orange Clips"

159

$\mathcal{B}$LETILLA
Bletilla

his superb dark pink orchid is virtually unknown in this country. Yet it can withstand Zone 4 winters for several years, at least in a large metropolitan area, even though the bletilla is often regarded as a non-hardy summer-flowering species.

As with the great majority of orchids, bletilla flowers last a long time and will enhance your garden for a whole month in the summer. Bletillas are natives to the cool regions of China and Japan. Their scientific name — *bletia*, of which bletilla is the diminutive — comes from Luis Blet, an eighteenth-century Spanish apothecary who imported the plant for his garden in Algeciras. There are a dozen or so species, but *B. striata* is the only one hardy enough to grow in the Great Lakes climate.

Winter protection

Like several other orchids, the plant grows from a pseudo-bulb, producing 12-16" (30-40 cm) long and lanceolate leaves, 1" (2.5 cm) wide, similar in appearance to the iris. The five or six flowers are located at the tip of a stalk 10-12" (25 or 30 cm) high. The "Alba" cultivar has white flowers.

In the flower bed, bletillas prefer a compost-rich soil able to retain moisture. At the same time the ground should be well drained and in dappled shade to protect the plant from direct sun. But even if experience suggests that *B. striata* is hardy enough, it's a good idea to protect the plant in winter with a proper mulch.

Bletillas can be cultivated in pots or put straight into the garden after the bulbs have been stored inside for the winter. Containers need generous watering in summer, but far less during winter storage. While the plant is growing, add fertilizer with every three or four waterings.

In the garden, bletillas will sometimes attract aphids. They are sold mainly through catalogues in the fall.

Bletilla striata *is a magnificent orchid that enhances any flower bed.*

$\mathcal{C}$ALADIUM
Caladium

$\mathcal{F}$ormerly considered only as indoor plants, caladiums can now be found in gardens during the warm-weather months.

Not widely popular as yet, they are becoming better known. Their big red, pink or white-splashed leaves light up the shadier corners of the garden.

Commonly called "Angel Wings" or "Elephant Ears," the seven recognized caladium species come from tropical South America, and their name derives from a local expression.

Leaves excite interest

Members of the *araceae* family, caladiums have large tuberous roots that produce characteristic flowers formed by the spathe and the spadix, rather like zant-

Martin Chamberlan, *La Presse*

Once considered to be indoor plants, caladiums can brighten up a garden.

162

edeschias, or anthuriums. But the flowers themselves are on the small side, without much aesthetic appeal.

Moreover, the plant has a habit of not flowering in the garden. No matter. The leaves are their interesting feature. They can easily be 6" (15 cm) wide and 12" (30 cm) long, and can grow even bigger depending on the type of cultivar and growing conditions.

Garden-variety caladiums are normally classified within the *Caladium bicolor* species, which has spawned more than 100 cultivars. The most popular varieties belong to the "Fancy Leaf" category.

Among others worth noting are: "Candidum": creamy white with dark green veins, green border; "Florida Cardinal": red center, broad dark-green border; "Fannie Munson": pink, laced with purple veins; "Florida Elise": pale green spotted with pink; "Mrs. Arno Nehrling": pink, veined in purple, green border; "White Christmas": white, dark green veins.

Mid-April potting

Caladium bulbs are generally potted about April 15. Once the stems are 8" (20 cm) long, towards the end of May, and before leaves have unfolded, the baby plants are transplanted outdoors, making sure to avoid direct sunlight. Pick a warm spot, out of the wind.

The soil should be enriched with compost and manure, adding in a little sand. Water on a regular basis but reduce the volume when the leaves start to wilt in late summer or early fall.

The tubers should be stored in vermiculite in a cool place, but never below 50°F (10°C). Immediately throw away any mildewed pieces.

In the spring, propagation is achieved by division, but keep in mind that the plant will produce four or five leaves before the colors appear.

With the exception of some tuber rot or, on occasion, leaf mould or spotting, caladiums are seldom affected by disease or insects. Florida is the leading producer.

$\mathcal{C}$ANNA
Canna

$\mathcal{C}$annas have become much more popular in the past few years, a growing infatuation attributable to an increasingly broad range of colors and the advent of handsome new variegated or streaked leaves.

Several recent varieties are less imposing in size than their parents. But their flowers are more prolific and bloom earlier than traditional cultivars, which often wait until the end of July.

Their popularity also stems from the speed of propagation and the ease with which this tropical plant can be grown. If the large canna rhizomes are placed in the proper setting, they will multiply significantly from year to year. A colleague of mine managed to produce about 600 seedlings within five years, starting with two large roots.

Even though there are hundreds of cultivars in existence, cannas are represented by just nine species, all native to tropical areas, from the southern United States to South America, by way of the Caribbean.

According to the standard classification, other authorities reckon that the number of species is closer to 50, some of which come from Asia. They are grouped together in the *cannaceae* family.

Canna *"Carnival Prince"*

Edible rhizomes

The name *canna* comes from Latin and Greek words meaning "a reed," a reflection of the plant's slender shape. Some varieties are capable of reaching a height of 10-12' (3 or 4 m).

These plants are denizens of hot and humid environments, and they produce large branchy rhizomes, some of which are edible. The green but frequently bronze-colored leaves — the inside red, or spotted with red smudges —

can achieve spectacular dimensions, stretching nearly 40" (1 m) in length and 6" (15 cm) wide. The leaves emerge from a sheath and rapidly unfold.

Flowers are located asymmetrically at the top of each stem on a spike that can be 12" (30 cm) long. They are made up of three petals joined at the base like a tube, with three sepals and several conspicuous stamens. The flowers display bright, occasionally mottled, colors, reaching up to 6" (15 cm) in diameter.

Plant indoors at first

Canna rhizomes should be potted towards the end of March to benefit from a long flowering period before the summer is over. Regular potting soil will do, but limit the amount of watering until the first shoots appear. Keep the plant warm and in sunlight.

At the end of May the canna may be transplanted in the garden, 4-6" (10 to 15 cm) deep, in well-drained, rich soil able to retain moisture, in full sun and sheltered from the wind. Leave from 10-18" (25 to 45 cm) between each plant.

Feed canna plants with a high-phosphate fertilizer every month. And remove the wilted leaves if you want to prolong the flowering period.

After the first frost, dig up the rhizomes and let them dry in the fresh air for several days before storing them in peat moss. They are often heavy, and always brittle. So handle them with care.

If the storage area is too humid, the roots will rot; if the humidity level is too low, they will dry out. So keep an eye on things during the winter months.

At least one bud

Separate the rhizomes in the spring, taking care to divide and keep at least one bud. You can also grow cannas in large containers.

Canna leaves tempt a number of garden pests, notably slugs, spider mites, and even caterpillars once in a while. The plant is also susceptible to rust and leaf mould.

The numerous cultivars are grouped together under the name *C. x generalis*, but are usually sold under their own name.

Several dwarf varieties belong to the Pfitzer group, not exceeding 18-24" (45-60 cm) in height. Still other cannas are listed in the "giant" category, reaching a height of 5-6' (1.5-2 m) in favorable growing conditions.

Some cultivars display distinctive features: "Lucifer": red flower, yellow border; "Picasso": red and yellow flower, reticulated; "Praetoria": green leaves streaked with yellow, very ornamental; "Stuttgart": pale green leaves, splushed with yellow; "Tropicana": leaves bronze-colored, streaked with purple; "Variegated Wyoming": bronze-colored leaves, streaked with yellow.

Jacques Allard

Canna *"Praetoria"*

Jardin botanique de Montréal

Canna *"Grand Duke"*

Jardin botanique de Montréal

Canna *"En Avant"*

CARDIOCRINUM
Cardiocrinum

Just imagine a lily that can stand up to 13' (3 or 4 m) high, with exquisitely fragrant flowers 8" (20 cm) long. This disproportionate plant emerges from a bulb of equally uncommon dimensions, the size of a cantaloupe. No doubt about it, cardiocrinum is a gigantic lily.

Members of the lily family, and native to Japan, China and the foothills of the Himalayas, there are three varieties of cardiocrinum.

The name derives from the Greek words for lily and heart, matching the outline of its heart-shaped leaves and the style of the flowers. *Cardiocrinum giganteum*, the most widely available variety, was once known as *Lilium giganteum*.

A recent publication by the Royal Horticultural Society refers to a specimen grown in England that reached a height of 10' (3.2 m), whose root stock boasted a diameter of 11" (28.5 cm). Each of the flowers was 18" (20 cm) long. Closer to our own backyard, Elsie Reford, founder and owner of the internationally famed Métis Gardens near the Gaspé peninsula in Quebec, managed to grow plants as tall as 12' (3.6 m) during the 1940s.

Anyone anxious to grow a cardiocrinum, as spectacular as it is, needs patience and a spirit of self-sacrifice. The plant dies after blooming. This specimen was photographed in the early 1950s by Elsie Reford, then owner of the Métis Gardens in Quebec.

Les jardins de Métis

167

A fatal blooming

C. giganteum is hardy in Zone 4, at least where the snowfall is heavy, but its size will be more modest than in its native habitat.

The leaves are rather large, from 16-18" (40-45 cm) long and a comparable width, but their dimensions decrease the closer they come to the top of the stem. In its natural setting the stalk reaches a height of 13' (4 m), terminating in a series of fragrant trumpet-shaped flowers — sometimes as many as 20. The white petals are occasionally tinged with green, and striped with maroon on the inside.

It is a strikingly beautiful plant, but short-lived. The problem is, that after it blooms, cardiocrinum expires and the bulb disappears, leaving a few bulblets in its place. These in turn will take from three to five years before producing flowers of their own.

Should you decide to use seedlings — a method of propagation that is said to produce stronger plants — you'll have to wait for seven years before they flower. Normally the flowers will bloom in late summer, leaving behind a profusion of seeds.

Under these circumstances, it's best to work out a planting timetable, using bulblets and seeds, so that you can have flowers every year. Cardiocrinum bulbs are costly, however, besides obliging the gardener to wait a very long time before they make the first and last performance of their lives.

Requires special preparation

Planting a cardiocrinum takes preparation worthy of the plant. First of all, you dig a hole 2' (60 cm) deep and 3' (1 m) wide, in which you put compost-rich soil mixed with ground-up leaves and some gravel to facilitate drainage. The location should be partly shady and protected from the wind. Then insert the bulb in its customized garden, making sure the top of the bulb is level with the surface of the soil.

The plant will thrive on a good dose of fertilizer high in potassium. The bulb can attract the greedy attention of squirrels, mice, slugs, and — who knows? — even your neighbors. Lily beetles also have a taste for the leaves — a major challenge for the majestic cardiocrinum.

COLOCASIA

Taro

*I*f you can't find colocasia at your local nursery — which wouldn't be surprising — or if the catalogue prices seem too high, pay a visit to the fruit and vegetable counter at a Chinese grocery.

The plant is better known by its Polynesian name of *taro* than as *Colocasia*, a term of Arabic origin. The rounded tuber, often bigger than a Spanish onion, is an important source of carbohydrates in the diet of several Asian countries.

In the garden, colocasia is grown for its broad green leaves, 2' (60 cm) long and 18" (45 cm) wide. At a height of 5-6' (1.5-2 m), the plant is an exotic presence in the flower bed.

The taro adds a tropical touch to the garden.

Jardin botanique de Montréal

In the water garden

You can buy the tubers in the spring and plant them indoors in a large container before transplanting them out of doors in May, at least 6" (15 cm) deep, when all risk of frost has gone.

Colocasia prefers a rather heavy moisture-retaining soil, rich in organic materials like compost or a well-decayed manure, in a shady location. It relishes hot temperatures but needs a lot of watering. In return, when the growing period really gets under way, you'll almost see it develop right under your very eyes.

Taros are also sold for use in aquatic gardens. They will grow in water provided that only their roots are submerged.

Leaves are the key

There are six species of colocasia. They come from tropical Asia and belong to the *aracea* family, like Jack-in-the-pulpit and zantedeschia. When cultivated for horticultural purposes, *Colocasia esculenta* will sometimes produce flowers in July, but several cultivars never flower. But that's of minor importance since they are principally grown for their tropical-style foliage. The cultivars are sold for the sake of their leaf coloring.

In the flower bed it's necessary to dig up the bulbs at the end of the fall and store them in a cool place. Plants that have grown in an aquatic environment can be kept in the house during the winter, say, in a bowl of water, in a bright location.

Colocasias are susceptible to whitefly, spider mites and thrips.

CROCOSMIA

Crocosmia, Montbretia

Dainty, lavishly blossomed, still quite unknown, crocosmias set the garden ablaze early in July.

Not only do several varieties make excellent cut flowers, but the flowering period itself lasts from four to five weeks. Small, ornamental green berries then make their appearance and last until the first frost if the stalk is not cut.

Crocosmias belong to the iris family and are also known as Montbretia. Together they constitute seven species. There are about a dozen cultivars. The name is of Greek origin and originally described the smell of saffron produced by the dried flowers after they have been soaked in water. The plant is native to South Africa and is considered a perennial in warm climates.

Internationaal Bloembollen Centrum

Crocosmias have spectacular blooms. They deserve a wider reputation.

Winter-hardy

On this continent, crocosmias are considered to be summer-flowering bulbous plants, although like the "Lucifer" cultivar, they can often resist the rigors of winter provided they're protected by a good mulch or snow blanket.

They can be planted in May when the ground is free of frost. The corms reproduce rapidly, beginning with underground runners, and are easily preserved in peat moss. Perennial corms, however, produce more flowers than those that have been transplanted.

The leaves are 1¼-2" (3-5 cm) long, linear, narrow and, often bent over. Located at the top of the stalk, the tubular flowers bloom one after the other, all the way to the tip of the inflorescence. Usually red, they resemble freesias. But the coloring also varies from a greenish-yellow to orange, and some varieties produce two-colored flowers.

The majority of cultivars sold by nurseries or catalogue are the descendants of *C. x crocosmiiflora*, a horticultural hybrid descended from *C. aurea* and *C. pottsii*, hardier than the original varieties. But *C. aurea* is sometimes sold as *Montbretia*, a name usually assigned to the cultivars.

Planted 4-6" (10-15 cm) deep, crocosmias prefer a soil enriched with organic material, in sunny, well-drained positions. Multiplication is carried out by separating the corms in the fall, when they're ready to be stored for the winter.

The plant is not subject to disease, but the leaves are sometimes affected by botrytis. Commercial production is concentrated in the Netherlands.

CROCOSMIA X CROCOSMIIFLORA

Montbretia

Origin: garden.

Flowering period: July.

Description: narrow, often spiky, leaves, 24-32" (60-80 cm) long. The stalk is often bent over, 24-28" (60-70 cm) long. Flowers are arranged in two rows. Color varies, depending on the cultivar.

Cultivation: easy to grow. Many cultivars: "Lucifer": bright red, one of the most popular and the hardiest; "Citronella": greenish yellow, at times reluctant to flower; "Emily McKenzie": dark orange with a red throat; "Emberglow": dark orange, shading to red; "Jackanapes": red and yellow; "Jupiter": yellow.

Hardiness: sometimes perennial in Zone 5.

ANOTHER VARIETY

Crocosmia aurea: 18-24" (45-60 cm) tall; flowers arranged vertically at the tip of the stalk, nearly perpendicular and opposite, more scattered than *C.* x *crocosmiiflora*; orange tones predominate.

International Bloembollen Centrum

The "Lucifer" cultivar is frost-hardy in Zone 5.

$\mathcal{D}$AHLIA
Dahlia

$\mathcal{T}$he dahlia boasts an impressive logbook. Before turning up in our gardens, dahlias were used for medicinal purposes, as a food, as an ingredient in human sacrifice — and even in plumbing.

Dahlias form part of the extensive aster family, and were first brought to Europe by the Spanish in the sixteenth century during the Mexican conquest. According to the Royal Horticultural Society, the Aztecs had long cultivated dahlias as fodder as well as for medicinal purposes, in particular for urinary disorders.

Native to the mountains of Mexico, and as far south as Colombia, dahlias were known by a number of names, including *cocoxochitl* — corresponding to *Dahlia imperialis*. This plant could grow up to 40' (12 m) high, and its hollow stem served as a pipe to bring drinking water from the mountains. Some historians suggest that the garland-like flowers were used to decorate the bodies of young girls who were sacrificed to the gods.

The "Marlon Amoroso" dahlia is a Quebec hybrid.

More than 48,000 cultivars

Early Spanish horticulturists felt that the tuber had potential as a food. In pursuit of this idea, Madrid's Royal Botanical Gardens began planting dahlias in 1789. Following experiments conducted in Spain, as well as in France and at Kew Gardens near London, it was concluded that the tubers were simply too bitter. The plant could be grown for its flowers, but not as a vegetable.

They also discovered that the plant was ideal for cross-breeding purposes. By the early 1800s, work on creating hybrids was well underway. And that's how the first double-headed flower was created.

Soon a veritable frenzy gripped flower-lovers, followed by a speculative craze that echoed the Dutch tulip mania. Tubers were being exchanged for diamonds.

The British National Dahlia Society was established in 1881, with a mission to mount botanical exhibitions and encourage cross-breeding development. Today, there are similar societies all over the world, devoted to every aspect of dahlia cultivation.

There are some 30 species, several of which have produced numerous cross-breeds. According to a California enthusiast named Gerald Weland, who has spent 60 years studying dahlias, more than 48,000 cultivars have been created in the past 220 years.

Related to the aster family, the flower was named to honor the eighteenth century Swedish botanist, Anders Dahl, a disciple of the renowned Carl von Linné (Linnaeus).

An unimaginable gamut of colors

The dahlia's tuberous root is easy to divide. It has big leaves made up of oval leaflets, notched around the circumference, and pointed at the tip. The leaves of a few varieties are tinged with red or brown.

Dahlias bloom in July and continue until the first frost. The flowers display an amazing range of colors and shapes, and are divided into distinctive categories that are used today as a means of classification. There are 18 such categories and new ones are added on a regular basis.

Worth noting, among others, are the cactus dahlias whose petals are rolled up over more than half their length and are reminiscent of a pincushion-like

Internationaal Bloembollen Centrum

"Joan of Arc" dahlia

Michèle Cartier

"Scarborough Ace" dahlia

"Scarborough Brillant" dahlia

"Hamari Rose," a ball-type dahlia

cactus. There are also dahlias shaped like pompoms, miniature balls, peonies, anemones and waterlilies. The orchid dahlias are among the prettiest varieties, due in part to their simplicity. Eight delicate petals, curled up and spaced far apart, surround the heart of the flower.

Dinnerplate diameters

The plants are also classified according to the size of their floral disc, the smallest one being barely 2" (5 cm) across. The largest of all are the so-called giant, or "Dinnerplate" dahlias. They can measure up to 10" (25 cm) in diameter, atop a stalk between 4 and 5' (1.2 and 1.5 m) high, sometimes more.

There are eight color categories. In other respects, plant size varies considerably depending upon the particular cultivar. Some are scarcely 12" (30 cm) high, whereas giant dahlias can reach a height of 6'8" (2 m). Smaller varieties usually flower more quickly.

Stake dahlias early

Dahlias do best in a well-drained, compost-rich soil, with a pH factor of 6.5. If the soil is too clayey, add sand and compost to facilitate draining.

When it is sold, the tuber should be firm. Make sure that the joint between the tuberous roots and the neck is intact. The size of the tuber has no effect on the height of the plant.

Around mid-May, plant tubers 5-6" (12-15 cm) deep, upright, adding a little bone meal or mineral fertilizer to the soil as you fill up the hole. Then place

"Marianne" dahlia

176

Michèle Cartier

Michèle Cartier

"Amy's Star," an orchid dahlia

"Little Showoff," ruff dahlia

a small stake near the spot where the bud is located. When the time is right, you can replace it with a bigger stake without injuring the tuber.

Select fertilizer carefully

The roots should be spotted roughly 12" (30 cm) apart. For smaller varieties the distance can be halved.

Choose a sunny, open-air position, protected from the wind. Avoid shady spots since plants need six hours of sunlight to produce generous blossoms.

Limit the frequency of watering. None at all until the first leaves have appeared. At that point water only if the weather is too dry. Over-watering can rot the tuber. When the leaves are fully deployed, give the plant a good weekly soaking, preferably in the morning to reduce the risk of fungus.

Fertilization is a key element in getting lush flowers. Balanced fertilizers such as 20-20-20 produce far too many leaves at the expense of flowers. At the start of the growing season, use a 1-4-2 formula and, in August, a half-diluted 10-52-10 solution applied every two weeks. Stop treatments early in September.

The bleach treatment

Dig up tubers after the first frost, when the foliage has completely wilted. Dig a shallow trench 6-12" (15-30 cm) away from the main to pull out the plump tubers that have formed during the summer. After cleaning off the roots with a hose, let them dry out for three days, leaving the stem upside down.

Next, sprinkle the tubers with an insecticide and fungicide powder, or simply dip them in a bleach solution, while the roots are being cleaned. The Quebec Dahlia Society recommends using 4 oz (125 ml) of bleach per 9½ qt (10 liters) of water.

Store the dry tubers in vermiculite in a cool and well-ventilated place. The use of peat moss is not advised because the risk of dehydration or decay is greater. Inspect the tubers regularly during the winter and throw away any that show signs of mildew. Mild cases can be treated successfully with a fungicide.

Division: a springtime job

When division of the tubers begins in the spring, keep a part of the neck when separating roots that have a bud on them. Then sprinkle with insecticide and fungicide.

You can also use seed, even though tubers offer a far greater choice of varieties. If you do, start the seeds 6 to 10 weeks before the final frosts. Seedlings usually germinate without a problem. It is sometimes necessary to pinch the stems to prevent unnecessary growth. Transplanting can begin at the end of May. As a general rule, seedling-produced plants flower sooner than those grown from tubers.

Insects and diseases

Slugs, cutworms, spider mites, aphids and the northern common rootworms all have designs on the dahlia. Viral and fungicidal diseases give the plant little respite either.

As for cornstalk borers, only a strong insecticide seems to do the trick. It's frequently impossible to treat diseases; it's better simply to get rid of the affected plants immediately.

Dahlias are commercially grown in a number of countries, but South Africa, New Zealand, England and the west coast of the United States lead the field in hybrid development.

EUCOMIS

Pineapple Flower, Pineapple Lily

The jaunty cluster of leaf-like bracts that tops the flowery spike of the eucomis gives it a surprising resemblance to a pineapple. Even though this unusual plant is scarcely higher than 20-24" (50-60 cm), it deserves a special place in the garden. The inflorescence often covers half the length of the stalk.

The plant is still not widely grown despite its attractive features and original shape. The flowers last through much of the summer. And when they're finished and replaced by a multitude of berries, the plant's beauty is unchanged.

Eucomis are easy enough to grow, even in pots. The bulbs increase in size over the years and can be safely stored over the winter months.

Needs breathing room

Aptly called Pineapple Flower or Pineapple Lily, the eucomis are among the many members of the lily family.

There are 17 species of eucomis, and they come from South Africa. Their scientific name means "pretty headdress," neatly emphasizing their crowning tuft of leaves.

The fleshy, rather narrow basal leaves, sometimes wavy at the edges, form a rosette measuring 2½-4' (80 cm-1.4 m) in diameter. The plant, therefore, needs plenty of breathing room. The spiked flowers are small, densely packed together — white, pink, purple, and sometimes white outlined with purple. Stamens are always visible.

Eucomis do nicely in full sun, in a rich, well-drained soil. Reproduce by dividing the bulblets or growing from seed. In ideal conditions seedlings will produce flowers in four years or so. Eucomis are relatively disease-resistant and free of insects.

Eucomis comosa

The bulbs are imported from the Netherlands and South Africa.

EUCOMIS AUTUMNALIS
Flowering period: early July.
Description: wavy-edged leaves, 18" (45 cm) long. Stalk: 18" (45 cm). Inflorescence: 2-6" (5-15 cm). Color: pale green, growing darker with age.

EUCOMIS BICOLOR
Flowering period: late July.
Description: leaves 12-20" (30-50 cm) long and 3-4" (8-10 cm) wide. Stalk: up to 24" (60 cm). Inflorescence: 2-6" (6-15 cm). Color: white with purple border. The cultivar E. *bicolor* "Alba" has greeny white flowers.

EUCOMIS COMOSA
Flowering period: mid-July.
Description: lanceolate leaves up to 28" (70 cm) long and 2" (6 cm) wide; the edge of the bract is tinged with purple. Stalk: 18-28" (45-70 cm), purple-spotted. Inflorescence: up to 12" (30 cm). Color: greenish-white, pinkish or purplish flowers, darker center. Formerly known as E. *punctata*.

EUCOMIS ZAMBESIACA
Flowering period: late July.
Description: narrow leaves 6-24" (15-60 cm) long. Stalk: 6-10" (15-25 cm). Inflorescence: 4-8" (10-20 cm). Color: White. The "White Dwarf" cultivar is readily available on the market. It has white flowers and is 8" (20 cm) high.

Jacques Allard

Eucomis bicolor

181

$\mathcal{F}$REESIA

Freesia

$\mathcal{F}$reesias' sweet heady scent, their wide range of colors and their longevity as cut flowers make them extremely popular with florists.

Year-round commercial production is aimed principally at the cut-flower market. The Netherlands and Japan are the major suppliers.

Unhappily for local gardeners, however, our hot summers are bad news for freesias. They need a very rich soil and plenty of water. If, by some miracle, flowers do appear, it will only happen towards the end of the summer. It is essential to use a stake or a trellis to make sure that the heavy floral spike doesn't make the delicate stem collapse. In a conservatory, the temperature must not exceed 55°F (13°C) if you want to obtain decent blooms.

On the other hand, some people have had good results by growing freesias in stone pots, set down in a cool place and exposed only to morning sun. Stake the plant in this case, too.

A metal trellis

It is astonishing how many retailers sell freesia bulbs in the fall, since the bulb is tender and cannot resist frost.

However, it is possible to force the bulbs indoors during the winter in anticipation of a spring flowering, provided the process can be carried out in cool temperatures, under artificial light. Freesias need several hours of bright light every day. The whole exercise will take three or four months, but, with good results, prove gratifying. The "Oberon" cultivar — red with a yellow center and pleasant scent — is an interesting candidate for this treatment. Here again though, the use of a metal trellis some 4" (10 cm) above the containers will help keep the stalks upright.

Members of the iris family, freesias are named after Friedrich Freese, a nineteenth century German botanist. There are a dozen species, all native to South Africa.

A bouquet of freesias, difficult flowers to grow in the garden.

Internationaal Bloembollen Centrum

183

$\mathcal{G}$ALTONIA

Cape Hyacinth

$\mathcal{N}$ative to the wet grasslands of South Africa, galtonias are herbaceous plants with white bell-shaped flowers that give off a faint perfume. There are three or four species. Belonging to the lily family, they are named for Sir Francis Galton, an English anthropologist and geneticist, and cousin of Charles Darwin, who travelled widely in South Africa.

Galtonias — or Cape hyacinths — are bulbous plants that flower in late summer. While considered to be tender bulbs, they are hardy in Zone 5, providing they are pampered a little by being given a good covering of mulch in winter.

Perennial bulbs produce more flowers

Cape hyacinths do well in pots. If you plant them in a garden, leave the neck of the bulb above the soil in order to reduce the risk of rotting. Some people, however, cover up the bulb to a depth of 6" (15 cm). Perennial bulbs produce more flowers than bulbs planted in the spring.

Multiplication can be carried out by gently separating the bulblets and also by seed. But the young plants must be protected from the frost for at least two months. Under ideal conditions, flowers will appear three years later.

GALTONIA CANDICANS

Cape hyacinth, Summer hyacinth
Flowering period: July, August.
Description: lanceolate narrow leaves, 20-40" (50 cm-1 m) long, growing from a rosette-like base, upright, but with pendent tips. Stalk: 40-45" (1-1.2 m). Flowers: between 20 and 30 pendulous flowers, in groups of 3, fragrant, 2" (5 cm) long. Color: pure white, green at the base.
Cultivation: light fertile soil, moisture retentive but well-drained, in a sunny position protected from the wind.

International Bloembollen Centrum

Cape hyacinths, or Galtonia candicans, *often flower in August.*

GLADIOLUS
Gladiolus

housands of years ago, in their wild state, gladioli were already being picked in some Mediterranean countries.

Historians now believe that biblical references such as "lilies of the fields" and "Solomon, in all his glory, was not arrayed like one of these" actually referred to the gladiolus.

Though some Eurasian species were cultivated in biblical times, the plant did not become popular until the end of the seventeenth century when the first specimens from southern Africa were introduced. Seven of these have since given birth to the majority of the modern large-flowered cultivars.

More than 10,000 cultivars

The name gladiolus comes from the Latin, *gladius*, meaning sword — the gladiator's weapon brought to mind by the flower's slender, sharply pointed leaves.

Gladioli are members of the iris family and there are some 200 species. They exist in a variety of habitats in almost every corner of the globe — from the Mediterranean basin, western Asia, Madagascar, the Middle East and parts of Africa. The largest number, however, come from South Africa.

The flower is constantly evolving, since even today there are more than 10,000 cultivars. And new, ever more beautiful varieties appear on the scene every year.

"Wind Song" gladiolus

Gradual blooming

Gladioli have slender, fan-shaped basal leaves, similar to the iris, from 10-36" (24-90 cm) long. The stalk may be as high as 32" (80 cm). The flowers are set vertically, pointing upwards, and are composed of six petals. They come into

186

bloom gradually, starting at the bottom. You can often find up to 25 flower buds, but 6-10 are usually open at the same time. A handful of delicate cultivars with a more "free" inflorescence often produce a mere six or seven flowers.

Constant attention

Gladioli require constant attention. They prefer a deep, light, fertile soil, rich in compost and moisture-retentive. But they also adapt well to slightly sandy soil, or even to a clayey soil as long as it has been enriched with compost, manure or peat moss.

The planting area should be well prepared, preferably in the fall, or if not, in spring as soon as the soil is workable.

Plant growth will be optimal in a warm, sunny position, sheltered from strong wind. Consider planting the flowers in a different spot each year in order to reduce the danger of thrip attacks — especially by the dreaded gladiolus thrip. Avoid planting the corms anywhere near vegetables, because the latter offer an irresistible temptation to thrips.

After buying corms, remove them from their wrapper, or tunic, and store in a cool, dry, well-ventilated place. It is also useful to give them a little anti-thrip treatment.

At the beginning of May

Plant them in early May, when the soil has started to warm up, in a furrow 4-5" (7-15 cm) deep, the biggest corms in the deepest part. They can be placed together in the middle of a flower bed, leaving a space of 3-4" (5-10 cm) between corms. On the other hand, in a garden set up in rows the furrows should be spaced at least 24" (60 cm) from each other so that a gardener can move around without difficulty when weeding and tidying up. Before planting the corms, check the flowering period of the cultivars so you can enjoy as lengthy a blooming period as possible.

"Her Majesty" gladiolus

Internationaal Bloembollen Centrum

Plant gladioli according to the flowering period of each variety.

Interval planting

Early varieties take as long as 75 days to flower in our climate, while the late-blooming cultivars will take from 90 to as many as 120 days. As for mid-season gladioli, the first flowers will appear from 75 to 85 days after planting. You can also get a longer flowering period by spreading the planting at intervals over several days.

Flower rows must be hoed regularly, a good chance to get rid of weeds at the same time. Some gardeners like to earth up the plants once the foliage reaches a height of 12" (30 cm), which helps reduce the need for staking the larger varieties. Mulching will help the soil to retain moisture and also keep weeds down.

Pick flowers in the morning

Gather up the corms at the end of September or in early October, when leaves begin to yellow, usually five or six weeks after the plants flower. You can also wait until the leaves are completely faded, since the corms will benefit from remaining in the ground as long as possible.

After removing the corms, get rid of those that show signs of age. Let the others dry out in the open air for two or three weeks and then eliminate the older corms. After cleaning, dust them with a fungicide, then put them in a container in a dry, ventilated spot. Any corms that show evidence of rotting during the winter must be discarded right away.

Gladioli are sold as cut flowers throughout the summer. Whether they come from the flower bed or the merchant, cutting should be done in the morning as soon as the second flower has opened up. Leave as many leaves as possible on the garden plant so that a new corm can take shape before the end of the summer.

A few fungal diseases

Gladioli are highly susceptible to a number of fungal ailments, and should be treated with fungicide all summer long. Thrips chew the leaves, making them wither and die. They even suck the sap from the petals, leaving them deformed. Aphids are also fond of gladioli.

Most of the gladioli grown in North America come from Canada, the United States or the Netherlands. In 1999, among all the bulbs exported to North America by the Netherlands, gladioli took second place, after tulips. The United States imported 220 million corms, Canada, nearly 20 million.

Jardin botanique de Montréal

"Aldebaran" gladiolus

GLADIOLUS CALLIANTHUS
Acidanthera

Origin: (Tropical) East Africa, from Ethiopia to Mozambique.

Flowering period: mid–August and after.

Description: upright lanceolate leaves, 18" (45 cm) long. Stalk: up to 40" (1 m) high, topped by a dozen scattered flowers. Flowers: pendent, very fragrant, funnel-shaped, about 2" (5 cm) in diameter. Color: pure white, greenish center, but dark purple in the throat.

Cultivation: like other gladioli, except this plant needs a little less water. Plant corms 4" (10 cm) deep. *Acidanthera* produce exceptionally beautiful and strongly, though pleasantly, scented flowers. A few years ago they were classified as *Acidanthera bicolor* or, more frequently, as *Acidanthera murielae*. They are always sold under the latter name.

Jacques Allard

Today, the magnificent and exciting Acidanthera *is classified among the gladioli.*

190

GLORIOSA

Flame Lily

Temperamental by nature, gloriosas produce strikingly handsome flowers under ideal conditions. However, the results may often fail to live up to those gorgeous illustrations in the seed catalogues.

There is just a single species — *Gloriosa superba* — and a number of variants. The best known is usually sold as *G. rothschildiana*.

Native to the tropical regions of Africa and Asia, growing in the forest or along river banks, the gloriosa is available as a tuberous bulb, cylindrical in shape and very elongated. The bulb will produce two to four stems that climb up by means of the tips of their small lanceolate leaves 2-3" (5-8 cm) which behave like tendrils on a stake or trellis. The stems can be 6½' (2 m) high, producing a number of solitary flowers, 3-4" (8-10 cm) in diameter.

An unusual beauty

Curved inwards at the top, wavy-edged, the six petals are a soft red, yellow around the border and across the center. The stamens are very long, topped by a yellow anther that stands out starkly from the center of the flower, giving it an unusually beautiful appearance.

You can cultivate gloriosa in a pot. The soil needs to be compost-enriched, well drained, fertilized every 15 days and generously watered during the growth period. Stop watering at the end of the summer when the foliage dies. The plant likes heat and a partly shady position. Some authorities recommend full sun, but too much sun will inhibit growth.

Internationaal Bloembollen Centrum

In the open air

Even though the gloriosa is not considered a true garden plant, it will grow out of doors alongside a fence, wall, or beside a trellis. Optimal growing conditions will ensure the best results.

Some people recommend planting the bulb indoors in a pot, and taking it outside only when the temperature is warm enough. Gloriosa bulbs are set in horizontally 4" (10 cm) deep. To multiply, separate the bulblets.

When purchasing bulbs in the spring, throw away any that are too dry. Keep them in their pot or in a peat moss mixture. Disease and insects are not serious concerns, but bulbs are occasionally ruined by rot.

Among *G. superba*'s variants, make a note of *G. superba* "Lutea" with yellow flowers.

Internationaal Bloembollen Centrum

Gloriosa rothschildiana *is a magnificent but capricious plant.*

192

HOMERIA

Homeria

omeria is a little-known plant, native to South Africa, of which there are some 30 soft-cormed species.

Homerias produce showy and fragrant cup-shaped flowers in peach, gold or pink, 1½-3" (4-8 cm) in diameter. Each stem carries several flowers, which open gradually. The corm produces linear leaves that are basal or attached to the stalk, often trailing on the ground. The stalk reaches a height of 8-16" (20-40 cm), and is sometimes divided.

Homeria corms should be planted 4" (10 cm) deep, in well-drained, compost-rich soil, with a sandy base, if possible. They prefer sun or dappled shade, protected from the wind.

Water frequently during the growth period, but gradually reduce the amount once the flowers start to wilt. For potted plants, stop watering completely after the flower dies, then store the plant in a cool, dry place for the winter.

To multiply Homerias, transplant the bulblets. It is virtually disease resistant and untroubled by insects.

H. collina is the most commonly cultivated species. Homerias belong to the iris family. The name has nothing to to with the Greek poet, Homer, but comes from the Greek *homereo*, "to meet," an allusion to the way the filaments of the stamens join together, making a capsule around the style.

Homeria collina

HYMENOCALLIS

Spider Lily

H*ymenocallis* looks a little like the daffodil. Its name comes from the Greek *hymen*, "a membrane," and *kallos*, "beauty," an allusion to the corolla uniting the stamens. The English, Spider lily, refers to the six long segments that encircle the corolla like spidery legs.

Hymenocallis itself is ravishingly beautiful, in spite of its comparison to an arthropod that is rarely appreciated for its good looks. What's more, the flower gives off a strong scent. It is often sold under the name *Ismene*.

There are about 40 species, found throughout North, Central and South America. A member of the amaryllis family, it is suitable as a potted plant and will flower in the garden as long as it is located in a warm, sunny and wind-shielded position. Flowers appear in July and last for three weeks.

Regular soil

Outdoors, the large bulbs should be planted 6" (15 cm) deep, in groups of three, if possible, in well-drained, regular soil. Frequent watering is advised while the plant is growing, but should be reduced gradually when the leaves turn yellow. Flowering normally occurs at the end of the season but can be speeded up if bulb growth starts indoors.

Dig up the bulbs in the fall, taking care not to break the roots, and let them dry in the open air in a cool place, where the temperature doesn't drop below 50°F (10°C).

For pot cultivation, place the bulb in a regular potting mixture, leaving the neck just above the surface of the soil. Begin steady watering when the plant starts to grow and use a fertilizer until the leaves turn yellow. Add a dose of potassium while the flower is blooming, as soon as the flower buds appear. Allow the soil to dry out in winter. Repot in the spring.

To multiply, transplant the bulblets. Hymenocallis are seldom affected by disease or insects. Commercial production is for the most part carried on in the Netherlands.

HYMENOCALLIS X FESTALIS

Origin: garden.

Description: 9 broad 2-2 ½" (6-7 cm), lance-like leaves up to 36" (90 cm) long — but often much less — upright but pendent at the tips. Stalk: 24" (60 cm), higher than the leaves. Flowers: 4 white, fragrant flowers, 4-6" (10-15 cm). The "Zwanenburg" cultivar is the most popular, white with glints of green.

HYMENOCALLIS NARCISSIFLORA

Origin: Bolivia.

Description: 6-8 leaves, fleshy at the base, about 24" (60 cm) long and 2" (5 cm) wide. Stalk: 24" (60 cm), the same height as the leaves. Flowers: 2-5, broad, up to 4" (10 cm) in diameter, white; the corolla is often streaked with green. "Advance" cultivar: pure white; "Festalis": white, the whorl of the corolla being pleated. Often sold as *Ismene* or Peruvian Daffodil.

OTHER SPECIES

Hymenocallis harrisiana: as many as 6 white flowers, delicate segments giving it a star-like shape.

Hymenocallis "Sulphur Queen": one of the most popular and sold under the cultivar name. Stalk: 24" (60 cm) high. Flowers: 5 or 6, bright yellow, with a large corolla streaked with dark green, 2-2 ½" (5-6 cm) in diameter.

Jardin botanique de Montréal

Hymenocallis *and its spider-like flower.*

$\mathcal{I}$XIA

African Corn Lily

$\mathcal{N}$ative to South Africa, ixias form clumps of very narrow, erect leaves from which the stalks emerge in May or June, each one bearing a dozen small, spiked flowers, less than 1" (1-1.5 cm) in diameter. The flowers are generally sold as a mix, but corms for individual cultivars are also available. Ixias make excellent cut flowers.

Members of the iris family, there are some 50 species, all native to South Africa. Closely related to the sparaxis, which have similar flowers, but larger and more showy, ixias share the same growing requirements. Their name derives from a Greek word referring to the flower's many different shades.

Ixias prefer hot weather and sunshine, like to be protected from the wind, and will grow in ordinary soil — alongside a wall, whose surface absorbs the heat of the day for example. If all these conditions are not met, then the results will be disappointing. It's best to take several corms and plant them 4" (10 cm) deep, placing them close to one another in order to achieve a handsome result. They will occasionally survive in Zone 5, but only with winter protection.

For pot cultivation, choose a container with a diameter of 6" (15 cm), fill with ordinary potting soil and place a dozen corms inside. Water and fertilize on a regular basis during plant growth, up to the time when the leaves begin to wilt after the flower has bloomed. Reduce watering in winter.

To propagate ixias, transplant the bulblets picked off during the dormant period or when the plant is dug up in the fall for storage. Seedlings take three or four years to come into flower.

Ixias are seldom bothered by disease or insects.

$\mathcal{L}$EUCOCORYNE

Leucocoryne

$\mathcal{S}$everal years ago the sole horticulturist still growing leucocorynes in the United States decided to give them up. But now the flowers are making a comeback in the North American market via the Netherlands.

The plant is a native of Chile and produces fragrant, star-shaped flowers in varying tones of blue. Each petal is smudged with a darker color and the center is usually whitish. The yellow anthers are clearly visible.

The delicate basal leaves are linear, often fluted, 16-18" (40-45 cm) long, fading during the flowering period. The 18" (45 cm) tall, crowned by an umbel of 6-9 flowers less than 1" (2 cm) in diameter.

Plant the bulbs 2½-3" (6-7 cm) deep in well-drained ordinary soil, in a warm, sunny position.

In pots or the flower bed

When planted in a pot, leucocorynes need water during the growth period, as well as a balanced fertilizer once a month while the leaves are out. Gradually stop watering after the plant has bloomed, leaving the soil almost dry while the plant is resting.

Propagation is achieved by the seed or by transplanting the bulblets taken in the fall. Leucocorynes are very seldom affected by disease or insects.

Only a single species is commercially available in Canada: *L. ixioides* . The scientific name comes from the Greek words *leukos*, white and *koryne*, club, alluding to the sterile anthers.

Internationaal Bloembollen Centrum

Leucocoryne ixioides

$\mathcal{L}$ILIUM
Lily

$\mathcal{L}$ilies are among the world's most widely cultivated decorative plants, harking back to the dawn of civilization.

Thousands of years ago, the tiger lily bulb — today a self-propagating species in eastern Canada — was originally grown as a food in China and Japan. Ancient drawings found on the island of Crete show that the Madonna lily had been cultivated in the region for at least 3500 years.

For Egyptians, the lily was the symbol of resurrection. The Greeks used the flower petals as a poultice for burns and snake-bite. The Romans liked to perfume their beds with the flowers. Lilies were also reputed to be useful for care of the breasts, for eliminating facial lines and wrinkles, and in the mixing of love potions.

Thousands of hybrids

Disseminated throughout Europe and Great Britain by the Romans, *Lilium candicum* (or Madonna lily) was venerated during the Middle Ages because it was associated with the purity of the Virgin Mary. Lilies began appearing in European gardens around the sixteenth century, at about the same time as the Canada lily crossed the Atlantic to be acclimatized, not without difficulty, in English gardens.

"Monte Rosa" Asiatic lily

Even though the tiger lily had been known in the East for a very long time, it wasn't until the beginning of the nineteenth century that the flower arrived in England.

And it would take nearly another century before a collector discovered in China the *Lilium regale* — the Regal lily, which was destined to become one of the most popular species.

The flower's name comes from a Greek word for the Madonna lily. Roughly 100 lily species are native to the northern hemisphere, including

North America, Europe and Asia. Some species are also indigenous to the tropics, but they grow at high altitudes. Today, there are thousands of hybrids and cultivars.

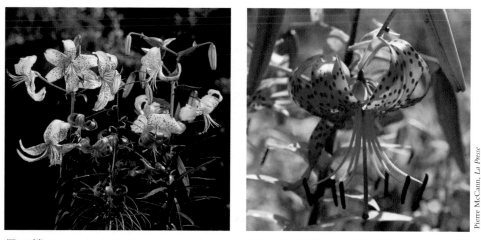

Internationaal Bloembollen Centrum

Pierre McCann, *La Presse*

Tiger lilies

Lilium lancifolium, *or* Tiger lily

Look out for the anthers

The linear — occasionally oval — leaves are usually glossy and spread along the stem. They are often set out at regular intervals, without a petiole and sometimes in whorls — that is, attached to the main stem, forming a kind of crown.

The stem is solitary, erect and not branched out, rising straight up from the bulb. It can be 80" (2 m) or more tall. The underground part of the stem is dotted with roots some distance above the bulb, and will occasionally form bulblets.

Classified according to their shape, the flowers have three petals and three sepals. The latter are the same color as the petals, but often slightly narrower. Six stamens are topped off by brightly colored anthers that can stain your clothes. Remove the anthers before putting lilies in a vase. The style is usually longer than the stamens.

The flowers open up one after the other, and blooming can last for several weeks. Cut the flowers whenever they start to wilt.

Cover well

Lilies prefer a deep, rich soil with a good admixture of compost or leaf mould, and decomposed manure.

Even if the instructions on the packet frequently suggest that the bulbs be planted at a depth equivalent to three times their diameter, it's preferable to bury them at least 6" (15 cm) in the ground, even deeper if possible — up to 12" (30 cm) — separated from each other by a distance of 6" (15 cm). A number of lilies, however, come equipped with contractile roots, allowing them to find their own preferred depth. Mix in a handful of bone meal as the bulbs are planted.

There are certain species, on the other hand, that need to be planted very close to the surface.

Fall or spring lilies?

When to plant — in the spring or fall?

In fact, the bulbs should be planted as quickly as possible after they're purchased. Fall consignments are often late. As a precaution, you should dig the holes as soon as possible, filling them with newspaper or mulch while waiting for the bulbs to arrive. If there has already been ground frost when they turn up, all you need to do is remove the material from the hole, put the bulbs inside and cover them with earth.

Planting can thus get under way rather late in the fall, even in December. During the winter the bulbs will become dormant, but will still be able to put out roots as the soil temperature permits. The following summer, they will flower sooner than lilies planted in May.

Lilies on sale in the fall come mainly from the western United States, particularly Oregon. Dutch bulbs arrive at a later date, because they're harvested later in the season.

In the fridge

Unfortunately, when bulbs arrive on the market in spring, they are often kept at too high a room temperature. As a result they start to grow rapidly. When you buy bulbs, select those with the firmest flesh. Then put them in the refrigerator, at 35-41°F (2-5°C), so as to lower their metabolism before actually planting them, once the ground has thawed. Early hybrid varieties will flower toward the end of June.

The superb Lilium pumilum *displays dainty foliage*

Jacques Allard

Good drainage is essential

While the plant is growing, spread some ashes on the ground or use a fertilizer high in potassium, such as a tomato fertilizer (7–7–10). The soil must always be well drained, because lilies absolutely detest getting their feet wet. If the earth is waterlogged, they are condemned to rot.

Frequent watering is not a necessity, therefore. On the other hand, the water has to soak down and reach the roots, which means that the soil must be slightly moist at all times. Water generously right after planting, however, so that particles of earth will stick to the bulb, and get rid of any air pockets.

Jacques Allard

The Easter lily is sometimes hardy in Zone 4.

202

Discard wilted flowers

For the most part, lilies prefer a sunny position, keeping their base in the shade if possible. Other species like a partly shady location.

Some lilies grow as high as 6½" (2 m) and need to be staked, at least in windy conditions. Be careful not to damage the bulb when placing the stake.

When blooming is over, cut the faded flowers but save the leaves. This is the best time to transplant lilies if clumps have become too thick or if you want to find a new spot for the flowers. You can also grow lilies in pots, but they need to be stored in a cold location during the winter.

Oriental lily, "Mona Lisa"

Jacques Allard

Separate the scales

Lilies can be propagated in a variety of ways. In the spring, seedlings can be grown in a pot. The young plants are then transplanted during the summer to a location protected from the wind. Remember, however, that hybrids that produce seeds will not produce identical offspring. To obtain an identical plant, it's necessary to resort to vegetative multiplication.

To do so, remove a few scales from a healthy bulb early in the spring and let them germinate in a clear plastic bag. Once the scales have produced a few roots and leaves, they can be transplanted. You can also transplant the scales straight into a pot after picking them. Some experts advise powdering the injured bulb with a fungicide to avoid any risk of infection.

The young plants must be fertilized with a diluted and balanced food and transplanted in the open air at the end of their summer growth period. Count on a few years before getting flowers.

Bulbils on the axils

Gardeners can also multiply lilies by transplanting the small bulblets that are removed in the fall after the foliage has wilted.

Some lilies, notably tiger lilies, produce bulbils on the axils of the leaves. Black or deep violet, they fall to the ground and quickly put out roots, forming a carpet of baby lilies if the situation isn't controlled. So plant them in an appropriate spot and then be patient — it often takes four or five years before you see the first flowers.

A ravenous bug

Lilies are besieged by a number of different insects, but the most ravenous is the orange lily beetle, which arrived from Europe a few years ago. This tiny creature looks cute enough, with its red back, black legs and antennae, but its voraciousness will soon dispel any tender feelings.

Orange lily beetles can devour a plant in a few days. Their larvae are covered by a kind of repulsive black slime. If you feel ecologically correct, you'll pick the bugs and larvae off by hand, but in a big garden it will often take several applications of strong insecticide to solve the problem. Lily beetles also attack fritillaries.

Aphids and viruses

Aphids, thrips and slugs all share a taste for lilies. The plant is also susceptible to a number of fungal diseases such as botrytis. In such cases, get rid of the tainted leaves and spray the plant with a fungicide. Viruses cause additional problems; and aphids are often their main carriers.

For this reason, lilies should be planted in the flower bed in small groups, separated from one another by bushes, large perennials or small conifers. These natural barriers will help to limit the spread of aphids and viral disease.

Complex classification

The lily market is flourishing and each year several new varieties are offered for sale. In 1999, the Netherlands exported 142 million bulbs to the United States and nearly 19 million to Canada.

Lilies are classified in nine groups known as divisions, and the ninth gathers all the species together. However, in order to make like easier for garden enthusiasts, lilies are also divided into three major divisions: Asiatic, Trumpet and Oriental hybrids.

Asiatic hybrids are thought by many to be the easiest to cultivate. They are descendants of East Asian species. They are seldom fragrant, often open at the top or perpendicular to the stem, while others are pendent. Their height varies from 18-48" (45 cm-1.4 m). Usually hardy in Zone 3, they are the first to flower — usually at the end of June or the beginning of July. Several have petals spotted with black.

Jacques Allard

"Aureliaar," trumpet lily

"*Star Gazer*" *lily*

"*Regatta*" *Asiatic lily*

Trumpet hybrids are descendants of Asiatic species and of the hybrid *L.* x *aurelianense*. They produce fragrant trumpet- or cup-shaped flowers, towards the end of July or in August, and are normally hardy in Zone 4, often Zone 3. One — sometimes nearly two — meters high, each stem bears between 12 and 20 flowers.

Oriental hybrids are the most showy. Their large flowers may be as much as 6-8" (15-20 cm) in diameter. Heavily scented, in tones of white or pink, the flowers are often spotted and edged with red. The most famous of the group is the highly fragrant "Star Gazer" which can reach a height of 4½" (1.5 m). These lilies can be more difficult to grow than others. They need a good deal of room in the flower bed and are not as hardy, despite the fact that they grow without difficulty in Zone 5. Propagation is slower as well.

Moreover, in recent years new lily varieties crossbred from *L. longiflorum* and some Asiatic hybrids have appeared on the market. They are known commercially as "L.A. hybrids." Hardy in Zone, 3, they display the coloring of Asiatic lilies as well as the shape — and sometimes the scent — of *Lilium longiflorum*, the

"*Inferno*" *lily*

206

Easter lily. They flower at the end of July and are 24-44" (60-110 cm) high. L.A. hybrids make excellent cut flowers.

Also extremely promising is a new series called **Orienpet** lilies. These are hybrids obtained by crossing other Oriental and Trumpet varieties. They produce very large flowers with prominent backward-curving petals similar to the Martagons, and their lengthy stamens give them a striking appeal. Hardy in Zone 4, they become even more resistant once they are acclimated.

The magnificent "Black Beauty" cultivar is often cited as an example of this line, but in fact it descends from two Oriental hybrids — *L. henryi*, and the red variety of *L. speciosum*. "Black Beauty" is sterile, but by crossing it with several varieties of Japanese trumpet lilies, the number of chromosomes carried by the offspring have been doubled, producing fertile plants.

Agriculture Canada has grown a few of these specimens at its experimental farm in Morden, Manitoba. They can weather Zone 3 temperatures without trouble, regularly flowering for three or more in early- to mid-August. Pay special attention to "Starburst Sensation," "Northern Beauty" and "Northern Sensation." Cultivars tend to be expensive and hard to obtain, a situation that will improve as production increases.

Agriculture et Agroalimentaire Canada

"Northern Sensation" Orienpet lily

LILIUM LANCIFOLIUM
Tiger lily
Origin: China, Japan, Korea.
Flowering period: July.
Description: from 12-20 lance-like, scattered leaves. Stem 24-40" (60 cm-1 m) high, sometimes taller, bearing numerous flowers up to 35 or 40, 4-6" (10-12 cm) in diameter. The petals are strongly recurved, pendent or nodding, without scent. Color: orange, heavily spotted with black.
Cultivation: sunny location or in partial shade, in which it will flower a little later. Produces a good number of bulbils in the axils. It is frequently sold under its old name, *Lilium tigrinum*. Often spreads beyond the flower bed.
Hardiness: Zone 2.

Lilium longiflorum

LILIUM LONGIFLORUM
Easter lily
Origin: Japan, Taiwan.
Flowering period: Easter, and at end of summer.
Description: numerous lance-shaped leaves, up to 7" (18 cm) long. Stalk is 12-20" (30-50 cm) high, at times up to 36" (90 cm). Fragrant, trumpet-shaped flowers, 6-7" (15-18 cm) long, endowed with a peduncle 4¾" (12-cm) long. Color: white. Some cultivars have yellow, red or pink flowers.
Cultivation: Easter lilies are grown in greenhouses for cut flowers and as potted blooms during the Easter season. They can be made to flower a second time, towards the end of the summer, if you cut the stem at pot level after the plant has bloomed, then transplant it in the open garden. However, avoid placing it close to other lilies for fear of transmitting viruses. The bulb is not recoverable after the second flowering.

This lily is not thought to be hardy in our climate, but some gardeners — even those in Zone 4 — have succeeded, with winter protection, in getting flowers for a number of years.

LILIUM MARTAGON
Martagon lily, Turk's Cap lily
Origin: northeastern Europe and Asia.
Flowering period: early July.
Description: lance-shaped leaves up to 7" (16 cm), borne in dense whorls. Stem from 40-60" (1-1.5 m) high, at times more. Numerous small nasty-smelling flowers, sometimes as many as 50, 2" (5 cm) in diameter, pendent, petals glossy and recurved. Color: pink to purple. The "Album" variety has white flowers. A number of cultivars are available.
Cultivation: slightly acidic soil, sunny or partly shady position, will also grow in the undergrowth. Flowering will often take from two to four years.
Martagon lilies are especially lovely and do well in a partial shade. The name "Turk's Cap" refers to their markedly recurved petals.
Hardiness: Zone 3.

LILIUM PUMILUM
Origin: northern China, Mongolia, Siberia.
Flowering period: end of July, early August.
Description: slender, delicate linear leaves, 4" (10 cm) long, covering the stem. Stem from 6-18" (15-45 cm) high, at times a little more. Flowers: 10-20 fragrant, recurved, pendent scarlet flowers, 2" (5 cm) in diameter.
Cultivation: lightly acidic soil, full sun or partial shade. Lily is often referred to as *L. tenuifolium* or *L. linifolium*. Also known as the Coral lily. A magnificent specimen.
Hardiness: Zone 3.

Jacques Allard

Lilium martagon

LILIUM REGALE
Regal lily
Origin: southwest China.
Flowering period: end of June, early July.
Description: scattered, linear leaves, 2-5" (6-13 cm) long. Stem from 20"-6' (50-180 cm). Broadly trumpet-shaped or bell-mouthed flowers — up to 20 or 25 — very fragrant, golden anthers. Color: pure white inside, pink or purple outside. Splendiferous! "Album": white flowers.
Cultivation: full sun.
Hardiness: Zone 4.

OTHER SPECIES
Lilium henryi: native to China. 5-6 ½' (1.5-2 m) high, at times more. Ten, as many as 20, flowers, petals recurved, orange, spotted with black, dark red anthers. Easy to grow in well-drained, lightly alkaline soil. Will wither away in an acidic environment. Zone 4.

Lilium pardalinum: native to Oregon and northern California. Height: 40-60" (1-1.5 m), sometimes more. A dozen deep orange flowers, pendent, petals sharply recurved, blotched and speckled with purple on a yellow ground. Known as the leopard lily. Moist soil, in sun or partial shade. Blooms at the end of the summer. Zone 5.

Lilium superbum: native to the eastern United States. Height: 40-60" (1.5–2 m), sometimes more. Flowers number 10-40, with sharply recurved petals, 2" (5 cm) in diameter, orange speckled with dark brown. Moist soil in partial shade. Flowers in August. Zone 3.

Jacques Allard

Regal lily

NERINE

Nerine

*N*erines are highly prized by growers. Their pink flowers stand up extremely well in a vase, and they grow as easily in pots as they do in the garden.

Nerine bowdenii *flowers at the end of August.*

Nerines belong to the amaryllis family and their 30 recognized species come from South Africa. Their name is a reference to the 50 daughters of Nereus, sea-nymphs who attend Poseidon, the Greek god of the sea.

Nerine bowdenii is the most commonly grown species. Its linear, glossy leaves are 12" (30 cm) long and 1 ½" (3 cm) wide. They appear during or even after the flower blooms.

The stalk is leafless and stretches 12-18" (30-45 cm) high. Grouped together in an umbel 2-3" (6-8 cm) in diameter are 6-12 tubular flowers, each equipped with a long peduncle and wide open at the tips. The stamens are long and clearly visible. The flowers bloom at the end of August. "Alba" produces white flowers.

Sunshine for flowers

Place the bulbs 4" (10 cm) deep in ordinary, but well-drained, soil, in a sunny location. Without sun, they may not flower. Store bulbs in a cool spot.

For potting, plant the bulb so that its neck protrudes above the soil. Water regularly, but not before the floral stem makes its appearance. Continue to water the plant throughout the winter and spring.

In May, you can put the pot outside in a partly shady location. Stop watering until a new stalk appears, usually in July. From the time that the flower buds show up until growth comes to an end, the plant will benefit from a regular dose of fertilizer low in nitrogen.

Repot only once in a while, because the plant will put out more flowers if it is closely confined. Propagate by division or by growing seedlings as soon as the seeds are ripe. There are dozens of nerine cultivars, deriving from several different species and specially sold for the production of cut flowers. They are classified according to height and flowering period. Nerines are sometimes called Guernsey lilies.

The plant is relatively immune to disease or insect attack. Slugs, as usual, are not so picky and will go after the leaves.

ORNITHOGALUM

Star of Bethlehem

Popular with florists because the cut flowers are long-lasting, ornithogalum is also an attractive garden plant.

The tender bulbs bloom at the beginning of August, and their pretty flowers are well worth the two-month wait, especially since they'll keep blooming for three to four weeks.

The variety *O. umbellatum*, known as Star of Bethlehem, is hardy in our climate and flowers in the spring.

Ornithogalum is a member of the lily family and is native throughout Europe as far as Russia, Western Asia and Africa. Commercial production is centered in Israel, South Africa, the Netherlands and the United States. The plant's name is based on two Greek words meaning "bird" and "milk," an allusion to the shape and color of the flowers. There are between 80 and 150 varieties, perhaps more, according to the official classification.

The shape of the leaves varies considerably depending on the variety. The flowers have six petals arranged like a white, yellow or orange star, darker at the center, clustered together at the top of a long stalk.

Tender bulb varieties should be planted in a pot or in a well-drained, sunny location in the garden. Plant bulbs 3-4" (5-8 cm) deep — twice that for *O. umbellatum* — in a moderately fertile soil.

Plants can be multiplied by seed, separating bulblets, or by planting the bulbils that form on the axils of the lower leaves. The sap may cause skin irritations.

Ornithogalum saundersiae

Jardin botanique de Montréal

Ornithogalum umbellatum

ORNITHOGALUM DUBIUM

Origin: South Africa.
Flowering period: August
Description: lance-shaped leaves, 4"
(10 cm) long. Stem: up to 12" (30
cm). Flowers: 20-25, 1" (2.5 cm) in
diameter, arranged in a pyramid–like
corymb. Color: orange or yellow,
the base tinted with green or brown.
Cultivation: easy to grow. Will
flower again in a pot.

ORNITHOGALUM THYRSOIDES

Chincherinchee
Origin: South Africa.
Flowering period: August
Description: narrow, linear, erect
leaves, pendent at the tips, 12" (30
cm) long. Stem: up to 24" (60 cm).

Flowers: Very numerous, arranged in
a pyramid–like corymb, ¾" (2 cm) in
diameter. Color: white, with yellow
center, greenish base.
Cultivation: easy to grow. This is
the most popular variety. Flowers for
three weeks to a month. Will bloom
again after flowers are cut.

ORNITHOGALUM
UMBELLATUM

Star of Bethlehem
Origin: north Africa, Europe,
Middle East.
Flowering period: June.
Description: numerous linear leaves
with a spot of white at the center,
12" (30 cm) long. Stem: 6" (15 cm).
Flowers: a corymb of 6 to 20 erect
flowers. Color: white with erect yel-
low stamens, greenish on the outside.
Cultivation: easy. Tolerates partial
shade.
Hardiness: Zone 3.

OTHER VARIETIES

Ornithogalum nutans: 12–16"
(30–40 cm) high. White flowers,
blooms in the spring, prefers partial
shade. Hardiness: zone 5, probably 4.
Ornithogalum saundersiae:
12–40" (30 cm–1 m). Spherical
corymb, white flowers with a black
or dark green center. Blooms in
August for three weeks to a
month, sometimes longer. A
magnificent plant.

POLIANTHES

Tuberose

Polianthes have long been admired for their spikes of waxy white flowers and heady fragrance — which some fastidious noses consider to be too strong.

Native to Mexico and the state of Texas, these flowers were grown by the Aztecs and used to add flavor to chocolate. They were also employed in the manufacture of perfume, especially in France and the Indies.

Members of the aloe family, their name derives from the Greek *polios*, grey, whitish; *anthos*, a flower. The plant's fleshy rhizome produces small bulblets every year.

P. tuberosa is the species most commonly sold by nurseries. Its narrow, linear basal leaves are 18" (45 cm) long. The stalk is 24-32" (60-80 cm) tall, topped by spikes of about 30 tubular flowers that have pinkish tips when they are in bud. Blooming generally occurs at the end of July and lasts two weeks.

Moist soil in winter

Tuberoses can be grown in the flower bed, but some people prefer to cultivate them in pots.

For planting in the house, use indoor potting soil, enriched with compost, and put the pot in direct sunlight or partial shade. As soon as growth begins, water frequently and fertilize regularly, until the foliage fades at the end of autumn or during the winter. It's important to keep the soil slightly moist while the plant is dormant in winter.

In the garden, tuberoses prefer a moderately fertile soil, well drained, and in a sunny, warm position. They will normally bloom at the end of July, but often later, at the end of August.

Reproduce with seedlings or by transplanting the bulblets in the spring. Commercial producers can generate as many as 800 plants from the sections of a single rhizome.

The plant is usually disease- and insect-free, but in cool or very wet conditions it can be affected by botrytis.

There are a few tuberose cultivars, among them "The Pearl," with beautiful double flowers. Commercial production is based in the Netherlands and the United States.

Double Polianthes tuberosa "The Pearl"

217

ANUNCULUS

Buttercup, Crowfoot

*I*t's hard not to succumb to the beauty of buttercups. They are a staple of florist shops. Their small, claw-like tuberous roots are sold in nurseries or from catalogues.

But while they are easy to find, there is also the potential for disappointment. Like poppy anemones, buttercups are very difficult to grow because our summers can be so hot. The plant adapts better to maritime habitats where summers are cool. In Mediterranean countries they flower in early spring, just as winter is coming to an end.

Jacques Allard

Ranunculus, *or buttercup, easy to admire but hard to grow.*

The plants can, however, be pot-planted indoors at the end of winter, then transplanted into the garden at the beginning of May, when there is no risk of frost. You may be lucky enough to see a few flowers eventually, but only if the soil is rich in compost and extremely well drained, and if the buttercups are growing in a sunny position. The jagged leaves will disappear rapidly after the flowers bloom.

The bulbs will then fall dormant, at which point the soil must be dry.

If the temperature is too high, the bulbs tend to rot. Should summer conditions be appropriate, however, the flowering period may be prolonged by planting the bulbs at intervals of several days. But don't be fooled: getting good results will prove the exception, not the rule.

It's a better bet to grow ranunculus in a pot, keeping the temperature cool — no higher than 50-60°F (10-15°C) at night — and the soil moist. The plant grows well indoors during the winter if kept in a very cool place 45-50° F (7-15°C) under artificial light. Stop watering after the foliage has wilted. The bulbs can then be stored in a cool place until ready for planting again.

The name "ranunculus" comes from the Latin diminutive of *rana*, a frog, because many species grow in damp places, or near the water. Some species are aquatic.

250 petals per flower

There are 400 species native to temperate regions around the globe. They are members of the *ranunculaceae* family. The species most commonly used by florists is *R. asiaticus*, imported into Western Europe from Turkey in the sixteenth century.

Since then, hybridization has proceeded apace. Today some double-flowered species and cultivars have as many as 250 petals per flower, and are much in demand. Buttercups multiply by dividing their bulbs.

Their leaves are susceptible to powdery mildew in hot, humid weather.

The most popular buttercups are variants of the "Tecolote Mixed" cultivars, which are 12-18" (30-45 cm) tall. Each stalk produces a big, solitary flower 2" (5 cm) or more in diameter, in a variety of colors, with multiple petals, and a blackish center.

$\mathcal{S}$PARAXIS

Harlequin flower

$\mathcal{T}$he sparaxis produces dazzling bouquets of brightly colored flowers. The center is usually yellow, encircled by a violet, almost black, border — usually in sharp contrast with the six petals, arranged in the shape of a funnel, whose color varies according to the cultivar. All in all, this presents a charming appearance. Some flowers display a very dark center.

Sparaxis tricolor, *known also as harlequin flower.*

Native to South Africa, the six species produce lance-like, basal leaves, similar to the iris and arranged in a fan. Each corm can produce several stalks 8-12" (20-30 cm) high, carrying between two and five flowers, 1¼-2½" (3-6 cm) in diameter. Blooming takes place towards the end of the summer. *S. tricolor* is the most common species.

Members of the iris family, sparaxis are also known as harlequin flowers. The name comes from the Greek *sparasso*, to tear, a reference to the frayed shape of their bracts.

Sunshine and warm weather

Sparaxis and ixias are closely related and share the same growing requirements. They will prosper in ordinary soil but in a bright, sunny location protected from the wind — beside a wall, for example. Should these conditions be absent, the results will be disappointing. To make things interesting, plant a few corms together, 4" (10 cm) deep.

A dozen or so corms can also be planted comfortably in a pot 6" (15 cm) in diameter in a regular potting mixture. Water and fertilize regularly during the growth period until the leaves fade after the plant has flowered. Reduce watering during the winter.

Multiply the plant by transplanting bulblets picked during dormancy or when the plant is dug up in the fall for storage. They can be kept like a gladiolus. If seedlings are used, it will be a few years before flowers appear.

Pests and diseases are infrequent visitors.

TIGRIDIA
Tiger flower, Peacock flower

Although a tigridia flower lasts only a single day, the sight is worth every fleeting moment.

T. pavonia, the best known species, and native to Mexico, produces large, brightly colored flowers stretching 2-3" (6-10 cm) in diameter, and more. The center is blotched, contrasting sharply with the color of the three large petals that form the main structure. Three smaller inside petals only add to the riot of color.

The speckled center of the flower evokes its name — *tigridia* — an allusion to the South American jaguar. Members of the iris family, there are 23 species, all native to Guatemala and Mexico.

Tigridia pavonia

Blooming in turn

T. pavonia, often called "peacock's eye," has lance-shaped basal leaves 8-16" (20-40 cm) high. The two or three leaves carried by the stalk are 24-32" (60-80 cm) high. In July, between three and six flowers open up in turn on each stem.

Tigridia bulbs are planted in the spring, 4" (10 cm) deep, in fertile, sandy soil and in a warm, sunny location. The greater the number of bulbs, the more spectacular the blooming. Bulbs multiply rapidly, and winter storage is not a problem.

There are several cultivars, but bulbs are usually sold as a mix, containing white, yellow, pink and red flowers. The plant will grow easily in a pot, but in this case plant bulbs deeper so that stems will be firmer.

Tigridias are virtually impervious to disease and pests, but the bulblets can be susceptible to viruses.

$\mathscr{T}$RITELEIA

Triteleia

$\mathscr{N}$ative to the western United States, there are about 15 species of this tender corm plant, which according to the scientific literature, cannot withstand northern winters. But for the past several years, my "Queen Fabiola" (a purplish-flowered descendant of *Triteleia laxa*) bulbs have spent the winter in the ground outside. Moreover, at certain times the temperature fell as low as 13°F (-27°C). "Queen Fabiola" is the most commonly grown cultivar. Each corm produces one or two linear, very narrow basal leaves, 8-16" (20-40 cm) long, that usually fade during the course of blooming.

And they are prolific. The stalk may be 16-24" (40-60 cm) tall. It is topped by a large umbel of up to 25 scattered funnel-shaped flowers 2" (5 cm) long. The flowers have a pale center and are attached to their stems by a long peduncle.

Gathering corms

In the spring, plant corms together in groups, 3" (8 cm) deep, in rich, sandy soil, in a warm sunny spot, protected from the wind.

Potted plants should be watered from time to time until the first leaves begin to show. Follow by watering and fertilizing once a month, with a balanced plant food, diluted by half. After the flowers have bloomed, gradually stop watering and store the pot at room temperature, keeping it dry.

The name *triteleia* is derived from two Greek roots alluding to the fact that the flowers sometimes appear in groups of three.

Propagate "Queen Fabiola" by transplanting the bulblets. The plant is relatively free of disease and pests, but is sometimes susceptible to rust.

T. laxa is often sold as *Brodiacea laxa*, its old scientific name.

Triteleia laxa

Internationaal Bloembollen Centrum

223

ZANTEDESCHIA

Calla lily, Arum lily

The growing of calla lilies — the popular name for zantedeschias — represents a veritable industry in itself. New Zealand leads the world in the export of this beautiful, tropical-looking flower, but it is also cultivated in the Netherlands, the United States, Japan, Italy, South Africa, Kenya, Mexico, Colombia and Costa Rica, to name only a few countries. Here at home, flowering pots and calla lily bulbs have become increasingly popular in recent years, due in large measure to falling prices.

Jack-in-the-pulpit's cousin

Calla lilies are members of the arum family, like the Jack-in-the-pulpit, and are native to the African continent, particularly the southern regions. Their scientific name honors the early nineteenth century Italian botanist, Giovanni Zantedeschi.

Still known today as the cally lily — the plant has had other popular names — probably derived from *Calla Palustris*, an aquatic plant found in the northern hemisphere (Europe, North America), which it slightly resembles.

Zantedeschias are distinguished by their spadix, a rigid, spiked inflorescence enclosed by a colorful spathe, or modified leaf. The spadix is located at the top of a stalk, which carries lance- or heart-shaped leaves that are fixed to the end of the rhizome.

Speckled with different colors, the leaves are extremely ornamental.

Calla lily "Black-eyed Beauty"

A semi-aquatic habitat

In their native state, calla lilies grow in a variety of habitats, but the largest and best known — *Z. aethiopica* — with a creamy white spathe, is semi-aquatic. This species has been naturalized in wet areas of several tropical countries, particularly in South America. It is fragrant. Bulbs are sold in the fall for growing indoors.

At present there are more than 100 zantedeschia cultivars, a few dozen of which are available commercially. Some species are sold under their original names: *Z. albomaculata*, ivory white, 20-24" (50-60 cm) high; *Z. elliottiana*, bright yellow, 20-24" (50-60 cm) high; *Z. rehmannii*, pink,

Zantedeschia aethiopica

Internationaal Bloembollen Centrum

14-20" (35-50 cm) high, at times up to 32" (80 cm); *Z. pentlandii*, dark yellow, about 24" (60 cm) high. All have produced their own cultivars, which are sold as such.

Three-week flowering period

Zantedeschias can be grown in pots or in the garden. As a potted plant, the rhizome must be planted in soil containing peat moss, sand and a little sphagnum moss to retain moisture. Water regularly once leaves appear and use a balanced fertilizer every two weeks.

Blooming will last about three weeks. The plant may be left to dry out at the end of the summer, or be kept in slightly moist soil during winter storage.

The rhizomes will enlarge quickly if they are fertilized on a regular basis and will continue to flower for several years. The bigger they are, the more numerous the flowers. If they're on the small side, the flowers won't appear for a year or two, or half-heartedly at best.

Many attractive cultivars

In the flower bed, plant rhizomes or young roots 4" (10 cm) deep in moist, compost-rich soil, in full sun or partial shade.

The plant can be multiplied by using seedlings (or seed) taken from the spadix — at least where fertile and hybrid species are concerned — or by gently removing the outgrowths from the main rhizome. The foliage is susceptible to a number of viruses.

In addition to the species already mentioned, here is a list of attractive cultivars: "Bridal Blush," pale pink with greenish markings; "Elegance": dark pink tending to red, delicate white border; "Treasure": yellow mottled with pink; "Cameo": peach yellow, turning to black at the center; "Flame": gold with hints of red; "Compact Flame": red with hints of yellow; "Garnet

A bouquet of calla lilies

226

Glow": dark pink; "Cream Lavender": pink; "Yellow Mammoth": yellow, oversize spathe; "Black Forest": purple; "Red Shade": red.

The handsome bright yellow Zantedeschia elliottiana *is often sold under its original name.*

ZEPHYRANTHES

Rain lily, Zephyr lily, Rainflower

ative to the southern United States and South America via the Caribbean and Central America, zephyranthes are tender-bulb plants that usually bloom in July or August.

Members of the amaryllis family, there are approximately 70 species. Their name comes from the Greek words *zephyros*, "the west wind"; and *anthos*, a "flower" — an allusion to their origin in the American West.

The plant emerges from a small bulb, producing very narrow basal leaves. The stalk measures from 4-6" (10-15 cm) high and is crowned by a solitary flower with six petals, 2-3" (5-6 cm) in diameter, and very long stamens. Colors vary from white to yellow, red to pink.

Zephyranthes should be planted 4" (10 cm) deep in well-drained soil, enriched with compost or well-decayed manure that will retain moisture even during hot summer days. The plants require a warm, sunny position. After the flowers have bloomed, add an extra filling of manure. The plant is winter-hardy in Zone 5 if covered with a mulch.

The flowers do well in pots, with maintenance similar to that of the amaryllis. Thanks to the proliferation of bulblets, the plant expands rapidly. Zephyranthes are rarely affected by disease or insects.

ZEPHYRANTHES CANDIDA
Origin: Argentina, Uruguay.
Flowering period: July.
Description: narrow leaves, up to
12" (30 cm) long. Stalk: up to 8"
(20 cm) high. Flower: solitary,
6 petals from 1 ½-2" (4-5 cm) in
diameter, resembling the crocus.
Color: white, greenish at the base.
At times the outside of the petals is
tinted with pink.

OTHER SPECIES
Zephyranthes robusta: normally
sold under this name, the plant is
classified today as *Habranthus robustus*,
a genus closely related to zephyranthes whose growing needs are the
same. It's advisable, however, to leave
the neck of the bulb just above the
soil. The stalk is 8" (20 cm) tall, or
more, with pale pink flowers.
Zephyranthes rosea: native to the
West Indies, especially Cuba. Stalk:
6-8" (15-20 cm) tall. Pink tubular
flowers with long stamens.

Internationaal Bloembollen Centrum

Zephyranthes robusta *is classified today among the* Habranthus.

Colchicum
Crocus
Lycoris

Autumn

$\mathscr{C}$OLCHICUM
Naked Ladies, Meadow Saffron

$\mathscr{W}$hat wonderful flowers! Just when we expect nothing else from the flower bed, when it's starting to look drab and colorless, up spring the colchicums, creating a mass of bright pink bouquets.

Their five or six cup-shaped flowers are borne on a short leaf less stalk 6" (15 cm) tall at the most. Blooms will last for more than two weeks, but the flowers tend to trail along the ground.

Members of the lily family, colchicums get their name from Colchis, a Black Sea region of Georgia. The flowers have long been recognized for their healing properties. There are about 50 species native to eastern Europe, North Africa and a number of western Asian countries.

Unwieldy leaves

Colchicums usually put out their leaves ahead of the flowers. In northern climates, the leaves — which have no aesthetic appeal — appear in the spring and may linger until they disappear in July. There are between four and six and they are hard to ignore — 12-14" (30-35 cm) long and 1½-2 ¾" (4-7 cm) wide — often erect, linear but occasionally lance-shaped. When planting colchicum, it's best to keep their sometimes awkward presence in mind.

Colchicum bulbs go on sale towards the end of August or in early September, when they are just about to flower. It's important, therefore, to put them in the ground quickly, in bunches of three or five, at least 6" (15 cm) deep in rich, well-drained soil, but able to retain moisture, in a sunny position.

Colchicums will multiply by seed or by dividing the clumps during dormancy — a delicate procedure if you wish to avoid harming the bulbs. Naturally enough, the young plants will increase in size. Every part of this plant is toxic and the bulbs may cause skin irritations when handled.

Colchicum autumnale

Colchicums are largely impervious to disease and garden pests. Production is concentrated in the Netherlands.

COLCHICUM AUTUMNALE
Autumn Crocus

Origin: Europe.

Flowering period: end of September.

Description: bulb is 2½-2¾" (6-7 cm) in diameter with a thick, brown tunic. Leaves: 3-5 linear leaves, 12-14" (30-35 cm) long. Stalk: 4-6" (10-15 cm). Flowers: cup-shaped, 4-6, in a bouquet, petals 1½-2½" (4-6 cm) long. Color: bright pink.

Cultivation: easy. "Album": white flowers, but smaller; "Alboplenum": double flowers; "Plenum": pink double flowers.

Hardiness: Zone 4, probably 3.

Colchicum *"Waterlily"*

OTHER SPECIES

Colchicum bornmuelleri: very narrow leaves, up to 10" (25 cm). Flower: dark pink or purple, white center. Zone 4.

Colchicum cilicicum: leaves 12-16" (30-40 cm) long. Flowers: numerous, as many as 20, lilac or dark pink. Zone 4.

Colchicum speciosum: leaves 7-10" (18-25 cm) long, 2-3½" (5-9 cm) wide. Flowers: large, cup-shaped, petals up to 3" (8 cm) long. Color: bright pink, whitish center. "Album": large white flowers, greenish center. Zone 4. "Water Lily": double, rose-lilac, often sold under its cultivar name, less hardy, Zone 5.

Colchicum speciosum

CROCUS

Crocus

*I*n North America there are at least five species of autumn crocus for sale at nurseries or from catalogues, among them the lilac-flowered *Crocus sativus*, the plant that produces the well-known yellow dye, saffron. Moreover, the color mauve predominates autumn-flowering crocuses, though some species have blue or white flowers. All of them put on their show in late September and early October at a time when flower beds are mostly bare. They are quite hardy and easy enough to grow in well-drained, ordinary soil. They like a sunny location, although some varieties will tolerate relatively moist and shady environments during the summer.

Leaves are delicate and linear, and appear in the spring only to disappear during the course of the summer. It's a good idea, therefore, to put them where they can blend in with the surrounding vegetation, while making sure that their flowers will be clearly visible in the fall.

4000 B.C.

C. sativus is the best known crocus of them all, and its use extends far back in antiquity. A fresco discovered on the island of Crete depicted a saffron gatherer. It was dated around 4000 B.C., an era when the stigmas were used to obtain an orange-yellow dye.

A thousand years later, saffron was being used as a medicine in Kashmir. It served as a narcotic, inducing a deep sleep.

Saffron comes from the Arabic, *zafaran*, meaning yellow. As for crocus, the name derives from the Greek, *krokos*, meaning saffron. So there you are.

The tips of the stigmas are harvested by hand. It takes between 70,000 and 130,000 flowers to obtain a kilogram of dry saffron.

Produced in Iran

Used for cooking, both for color and for flavor, saffron is produced in several countries, among them Spain, India and, to a lesser extent, some European countries. Iran is the most important producer. Autumn crocuses come mainly from the Netherlands, as is the case with the majority of spring-flowering species.

Crocus sativus is reproduced exclusively by offsets picked when the plant is dormant. Other species reproduce by seed, but the process can be carried out more straight-forwardly simply by dividing the clumps when they grow too thick.

Like those that bloom in spring, autumn crocuses are susceptible to a whole host of diseases that have little impact on the garden. Mice and squirrels, on the other hand, like nothing better on their menu, and can cause severe problems.

Crocus sativus, *the saffron-producing species.*

Internationaal Bloembollen Centrum

CROCUS KOTSCHYANUS

Origin: Turkey, Syria, Lebanon.
Flowering period: mid-September.
Description: 4-5 leaves, produced after flowering. Flower: solitary, tubular at the base, cup-shaped. Color: pale bluish-pink, yellow in the center. Total height: 2½-4" (6-10 cm).
Cultivation: well-drained, moist soil, dryer in mid-summer, partial shade. Often sold as *C. zonatus*.
Hardiness: Zone 4.

CROCUS SATIVUS

Saffron crocus
Origin: uncertain, possibly a hybrid of a native Greek species.
Flowering period: September.
Description: 1-5 lilac-colored flowers. Total height: 2½-4" (7-10 cm). Flowering lasts 2-3 weeks.
Cultivation: well-drained soil, warm and sunny location. Will grow in moderately moist soil. Usually blooms during the second or third year after planting because bulbs sold in northern U.S.A. and Canada tend to be smaller. Will not flower if temperatures are too cold.
Hardiness: Zone 4.

CROCUS SPECIOSUS

Origin: Turkey, Iran, Russia.
Flowering period: October.
Description: 3-5 leaves, produced after flowering. Stalk: up to 6" (15 cm). Flower: solitary, mauve, very pretty.
Cultivation: similar to *C. kotschyanus*. "Albus": white flowers; "Conqueror": dark blue.
Hardiness: Zone 4

OTHER SPECIES

Crocus goulimyi: one or two very pale blue flowers. Plant in sun or partial shade. Flowers at the end of September. Zone 4, probably 3.
Crocus pulchellus: very pale blue flowers with darker lines, yellow center. Flowers at the end of September. Zone 5, probably 4.

$\mathcal{L}$YCORIS

Lycoris, Golden Spider Lily

$\mathcal{S}$ometimes also affecetionately called "naked ladies," lycoris are said to be named after a beautiful Roman actress who was once the mistress of Mark Antony.

A member of the amaryllis family, lycoris produces pretty yellow, red, orange, pink and lavender flowers atop a stalk 12-18" (30-45 cm) high. Native to China and Japan, lycoris is not regarded as frost-hardy.

Lycoris squamigera will, however, flower in Zone 4 in the garden, without protection, at least in an urban environment. It is available from catalogues.

Patience is a virtue

This bulbous plant comes from Japan. It produces lance-shaped leaves about 12" (30 cm) long and ¾-1" (2-2.5 cm) wide, that appear in the spring but last several weeks before disappearing.

Flowering occurs in September. The stalk then lengthens rapidly to reach 12-16" (30-40 cm) — sometimes double that in warmer regions — and is covered by a bouquet of six to eight fragrant flowers in shades of pink or lilac, with wavy petals, up to 3" (8 cm) in diameter.

L. squamigera can be grown in fertile, well-drained soil, in a sunny position and protected from the wind. Plant bulbs 6" (15 cm) deep and give them winter protection. You must also be patient while waiting for the first flowers to appear — it may take as long as five years after the bulbs have been planted, even though leaves appear each spring.

Lycoris squamigera

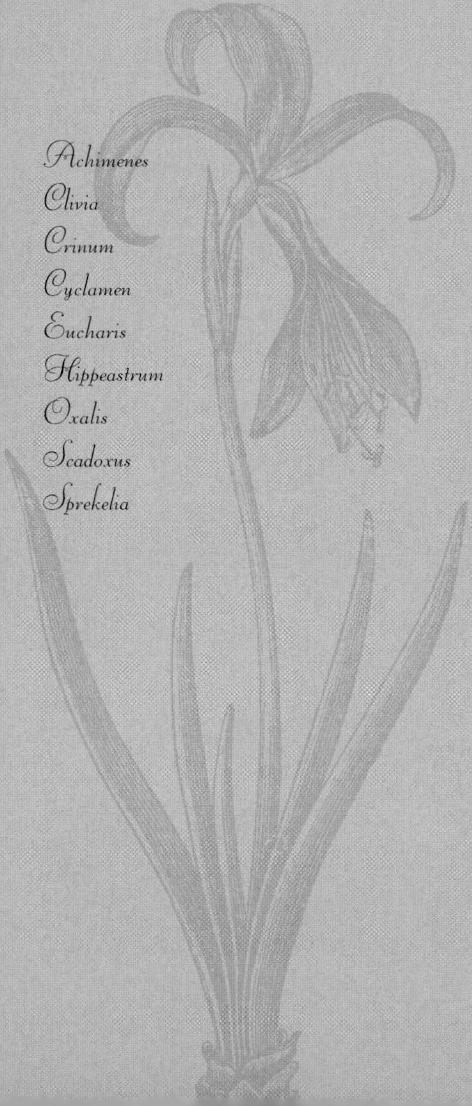

Achimenes
Clivia
Crinum
Cyclamen
Eucharis
Hippeastrum
Oxalis
Scadoxus
Sprekelia

Winter

ACHIMENES

Hot Water Plant

chimenes are indoor plants that make magnificent hanging baskets, offering an abundance of flowers for much of the summer.

Grown from a rhizome, they require little maintenance. Stems are usually 6-10" (15-25 cm) long, some times twice that for some cultivars. The tubular, trumpet-shaped flowers have a diameter of about 2" (5 cm).

Its colors are very diversified, due in large measure to the hundreds of cultivars developed since the end of the nineteenth century, many of which are descendants of *A. longiflora*. Like African violets, achimenes are members of the *gesneriaceae* family. There are some 25 species native to the West Indies, Mexico and Central America. Their name derives from the Greek word *achaemenis*, a "magic plant."

Sensitive to dryness

Plant the rhizomes ¾" (2 cm) deep in well-drained soil, at normal temperature, in bright or medium light, about a dozen per pot 6" (15 cm) in diameter. Start watering when the first shoots appear, keeping water temperature on the tepid side. Even a brief dry period will either kill the plant or trigger dormancy.

Fertilize the plant when the first stems emerge from the soil and continue until the flower buds appear. Achimenes may be put outside in a warm spot, but not in direct sunlight. In summer keep it in a moist atmosphere. Pinch off the tips of the stems to get a bushier plant.

Easy to multiply

Reduce watering after the plant has flowered. When the foliage wilts in the fall, store plant and pot in a cool spot. Repot in the spring and moisten the soil.

Achimenes can be multiplied easily enough by taking cuttings during the growth period, by separating the rhizomes or planting the scales that occasionally appear on the axis of the leaves. Growing seedlings is a more difficult enterprise.

Insects, especially aphids, can be a concern. Commercial production is based in Germany, the Netherlands, and the United States.

Achimenes belong to the large family of gesneriaceae, which includes African violets.

Internationaal Bloembollen Centrum

$\mathcal{C}$LIVIA
Clivia

$\mathcal{C}$livia's orange or bright yellow flowers emerge dramatically from a lush bouquet of fleshy, dark green leaves. They seldom go unnoticed among a shelf-full of other indoor plants.

Clivias are a rhizomatous species, sold as flowering houseplants in the spring. Looked after carefully, they will last for more than 20 years, flowering at least once a year. The thick, fleshy rhizomes can reach a considerable size, and will flower more extravagantly if kept in a confined space.

Once well established, clivias hate being disturbed. There is therefore no need to repot the plants; simply replenish the surface soil.

Green-flowered varieties

There are four species, all native to South Africa. The plant was named for the Duchess of Northumberland, born Charlotte Clive, granddaughter of Robert Clive (Clive of India), in whose English garden it was first cultivated.

The best known and most attractive species is *Clivia miniata,* or Kaffir lily. It produces numerous linear leaves 16-24" (40-60 cm) long, which grow out of the center of the rhizome's offsets. The stalk can reach a height of 16-18" (40-45 cm), and is topped by an umbel of funnel-shaped flowers 1½-2" (4-5 cm) long, orange with a yellowish center: The "Aurea" cultivar has yellow flowers. There are also a few large-flowered varieties with variegated leaves and dark orange or greenish flowers.

As they mature, Clivia miniata *flowers produce ornamental red berries.*

242

Slow growth

Use indoor potting soil, adding compost and a small amount of gravel to help drainage. Clivias like bright light, but not direct sun, and they need plenty of water while they're growing. Fertilize weekly until the flower buds appear.

Cut the base of the stem after the plant has flowered, unless you wish to help the red berries on the stalk ripen. Then gradually reduce watering, keeping the soil slightly moist in a cold place while the plant rests during the winter.

Clivias are slow growers. Multiply by dividing them up, or by sowing seed. It will take from three to six years before you get the first flowers.

The plant is susceptible to mealybugs. Sap from the leaves may irritate the skin.

Clivia miniata *will live for many years if properly cared for.*

243

Crinum

Crinum

Crinums belong to the same family as the amaryllis, with whom they share a number of characteristics, but they are less well known by far. There are around 130 species, native to South Africa and a number of tropical countries. But the most commonly available species is a garden

International Bloembollen Centrum

The crinum is highly prized by florists.

hybrid — *Crinum* x *powellii*. Crinum is taken from the Greek word *krinon*, meaning "lily," and it is best pot-grown.

The bulb is large, up to 6" (15 cm) in diameter, and produces arching, sword-shaped leaves, up to 60 cm long. The stalk is 24" (60 cm) high, more in favorable conditions, ending with 8-10 lily-like flowers with long peduncles, highly scented, around 4" (10 cm) long.

Flowering normally occurs at the end of summer or in the fall as far as younger plants are concerned, but it can also be year-long. A bulb may take two to four years to produce its first flower.

Green leaves throughout the year

The neck of the large tapering bulb should protrude from the soil as it is plant-ed. It needs a rich, slightly sandy soil, in a sunny location, but can stand the shade for a few hours a day. Water generously while the plant is growing, and fertilize monthly with a balanced plant food.

Reduce watering after the plant has flowered. Leaves will stay green as long as the soil is kept lightly moist while the plant is resting. Or simply stop adding water altogether to give the plant a complete winter rest.

Crinum can remain in the same pot for several years. Flowering will be more abundant if the bulb and the offsets are tightly confined.

Repot in the spring if need be. Should it be necessary, replenish the surface soil. Every part of the plant, including the bulb, can cause skin irritations.

Thrips and mealybugs can harm crinums.

CYCLAMEN

Cyclamen

Bright colors and a six-to-eight-week flowering period help make cyclamens highly popular houseplants. Our northern climate keeps them indoors, but you can also buy tubers, and at least one species — *C. purpurascens* — is perennial outdoors in Zone 4.

Cyclamens belong to the primrose family, and are native to the countries along the shores of the Mediterranean as far as Iran. There are 19 species. The bulbs have long been used as a vermifuge (worm repellent) and in the manufacture of ointment. The name comes from the Greek *kyklos*, "circular," after the spiraling movement of the stems, or perhaps the round shape of the tuber.

"Butterfly Rose" cyclamen

Reproduction by seed

Cyclamens were first brought to Europe in the late sixteenth or early seventeenth century, but their real popularity spurt began in Germany in 1870. There, geneticists created a number of much larger-flowered species corresponding to the modern varieties with which we are all familiar.

Today's hybrids are the result of generations of careful selection and breeding among several species, notably *C. persicum*, the so-called florists' cyclamen. The plants are sometimes grouped together as *C. persicum giganteum*, and produce fertile flowers, which makes them useful in commercial production of seedlings.

For the most part, cyclamens go on sale from September to May. They are not fond of heat, so too high an indoor temperature will often cause them to wither away. For this reason, it's a good idea to put the plant on a north- or east-facing windowsill. Room temperature can go as low as 54 °F (12 °C) without risk. Although photoperiodism appears to have little or no effect on the plant's development, nevertheless it's clear that longer days and brighter light help it to produce more buds.

Please don't splash me!

Another common mistake: over-watering. All you need to do is let the pot soak in a bowl of water for 20 minutes whenever the soil is dry. Then throw away the excess. You can also immerse the plant in water, but be careful not to splash the leaves in order to avoid leaf spotting. The plant should be fed once a month during the growth period with a balanced fertilizer or one low in nitrogen.

Cyclamens can remain in their pots for a long time, at least until the tubers start to take up too much room and inhibit the plant's ability to flower.

All cyclamens generally fall dormant during their yearly cycle, usually soon after they have flowered. Stop watering and fertilizing completely once the leaves begin to die down. This will last for two or three months until new shoots appear.

Carefully looked after, a cyclamen will flourish for an astonishing 10 — perhaps even 15 — years.

Some flowers are fragrant

It's best to propagate by seed, especially since some varieties are on offer from seed merchants. The "Scentsation" variety produces different colored flowers with a scent reminiscent of freesias.

Greenhouse varieties usually flower between eight and nine months after seeding. In the house, however, you'll need to wait between 15 and 18 months for the same results, although dwarf cultivars can flower in seven or eight months.

Aside from problems attributable to poor maintenance, cyclamens are relatively free from disease or infestation. The cyclamen mite can cause damage, however.

There are, incidentally, two species that are hardy in our climate.

CYCLAMEN PURPURASCENS

Origin: Europe.

Description: small, round, heart-shaped leaves, with silvery spots. Flowers: dark pink, 2 cm long, fragrant. Total height: 4" (10 cm).

Cultivation: soil moderately fertile, humus-rich, well drained, 4" (10 cm) deep, in partial shade.

Hardiness: Zone 4.

This plant has grown for a number of years without special care or protection in the town of Boisbriand, Que., under a spruce tree. The flowers form an attractive carpet. Still, a winter mulch will protect the plant

Cyclamen persicum *"Alouette"*

more effectively. This species can be purchased from selected seed merchants. It is sometimes classified as *C. europaeum*.

ANOTHER SPECIES

Cyclamen hederifolium: 4" (10 cm) high overall. Flower: pink. Available as bulbs. Hardiness: Zone 5 with protection.

Cyclamen indicum

$\mathcal{E}$UCHARIS
Amazon lily

$\mathcal{E}$ucharis are indoor plants from the amaryllis family. They produce heavily scented white flowers, occasionally two or three times a year.

There are 17 species and two natural hybrids, all native to tropical regions of Central America, extending to the Amazon basin and western South America. One of the best known species is *E.* x *grandiflora*, or Amazon lily, which comes from Colombia.

It produces from one to four oval glossy green leaves about 12" (30 cm) long and up to 6" (15 cm) wide. The stalk, 20" (50 cm) high, carries 2-6 white flowers, 2-4" (5-8 cm) across, looking rather like a narcissus. The stamens extend well beyond the corolla, although the style is still further projected towards the front. Eucharis comes from the Greek word for "charming," or "pleasing," refering to the flower's attractive appearance.

Keep the "nose" in sight

Plant the bulb in an earthenware pot containing compost-rich soil mixed in with a little sand, but leaving the "nose" of the bulb just above the surface of the soil.

Keep the pot lightly moist. Water regularly but moderately as soon as the first stem appears, something that usually happens fairly quickly. Flowering generally occurs three months after the bulb has been planted and lasts for about three weeks.

Give the plant a balanced fertilizer every week once it starts growing. Reduce watering in winter. The plant may be put outside in the summer in the morning sun, but keep it away from direct sunlight between 11 a.m. and 3 p.m.

Repot every three years

Once flowering is over, you can reduce watering and allow the soil to dry out a little. This usually prompts a second flowering.

As a general rule repot the plant every three or four years. By then there will often be a good many bulblets that can be transplanted. Eucharis is rarely affected by disease or garden pests.

International Bloembollen Centrum

Eucharis x grandiflora

ℋIPPEASTRUM
Amaryllis

*A*t first sight, it's nothing to write home about. The bulb is large and plump, with a brown, often frayed, tunic. A stout green stem emerges from the center, at times a little bent after storage. Everyone knows that bulbs don't like being kept with their heads down!

Then, once inside a pot, in bright daylight, before the roots get a good foundation, the stem straightens up. And in record-breaking time, from two to six spectacular flowers unfold, each 6" (15 cm) across. It's the amaryllis miracle.

And if you take good care of it, the plant will prove remarkably faithful, flowering over and over again, for 10, 15, even 20 years. Better still, it will quietly multiply in its container, and finish off by producing a huge bouquet.

A name based on a mistake
The amaryllis is not only easy to look after, but it stays healthy, and insects happily ignore it. And if you also take account of the different flower shapes, the broad range of colors, the delicate fragrance that some varieties exude, and the very affordable price, then it's easy to understand why the plant's popularity is growing.

The popular name derives from its close resemblance to *Amaryllis belladonna*, a South African bulbous plant related to Hippeastrum, which produces flowers similar to the nerines and crinums.

A tragic legend
A Greek myth relates the tragic story of a lovely shepherdess

Amaryllis *"Orion"*

named Amaryllis, who fell head over heels in love with a shepherd. Alas, the youth was more interested in flowers than he was in romance. It was said that he could only be seduced by a young woman who brought him a flower that he had never seen before. After consulting the oracle, Amaryllis turned up at the

251

Amaryllis *"Red Lion"*

shepherd's hut and wounded her own breast in an attempt to arouse him. Her self-inflicted pain was a waste of time. But still, the strength of her passion led her to keep up the mortal struggle for 31 long nights.

At the very last moment, a magnificent flower sprang from the blood-soaked earth, and the shepherd finally succumbed. The flower was called amaryllis.

The story says nothing further about the two lovers and doesn't tell us how the Greeks came in contact with *Amaryllis belladonna*, which, after all, didn't grow in their part of the world.

A hundred or more varieties

The great majority of the amaryllis with which we are familiar are cultivars bred from Central and South American species of the genus *Hippeastrum*, a term whose significance is unclear. It may derive from the Greek *hippos*, "a horse."

252

There are roughly 80 species in wet and mountainous regions, but fewer cultivated species, *H. papilio* being the best known.

Today there are a few hundred amaryllis cultivars, but only a dozen or so are commercially important. About 10 million bulbs are sold annually worldwide, and this market will certainly increase, given the plant family's genetic potential.

Amaryllis *"Apple Blossom"*

Crossbreeding in 1799

Amaryllis production is concentrated in South Africa, the Netherlands, Israel and, most recently, in Brazil. Most bulbs still come from the Netherlands, however.

Breeding and selection have been going on for a much longer time — ever since an English watchmaker named Arthur Johnson succeeded in crossing two species in 1799, creating an exceptionally prolific flowerer. In the much more recent past, crossings between *Hippeastrum* and *Nerine*, and between *Crinum* and *Sprekelia*, have also produced interesting results.

A question of size

In the past few years, several new varieties have appeared in the marketplace, particularly some stocks with smaller stems and flowers as well as double-flowered and fragrant cultivars like "Blossom Peacock," with pink and white flowers. There are a number of varieties in changing shades of red or pink, some a greenish-yellow, others peach or orangey. "Picotee" is white, with a delicate red border around the petals.

An amaryllis stalk can reach a height of 12-20" (30-50 cm), and carry from two to six flowers. Made up of six large petals, the flowers are trumpet-shaped, wide open at the mouth, and feature six long, clearly visible stamens.

As a general rule, the bigger the bulb, the more it will cost, and the greater the number of stalks. But some new cultivars of equal size are just as prolific.

Internationaal Bloembollen Centrum

Amaryllis *"Picotee,"* in all its splendor.

A warm bath

Amaryllis are grown in a container filled with regular potting soil or a sterilized mixture containing sphagnum moss and perlite — about 60 percent. Leave the upper part of the bulb — its so-called "shoulders" — exposed, and handle the roots gently.

It is advisable to use a pot 1½-2½" (4-6 cm) wider than the bulb. An earthenware or stone pot is preferable to plastic, but even it can be too heavy and cumbersome. Some people grow their *Hippeastrum* in big stone pots 10" (25 cm) in diameter to give the bulbs plenty of expansion room and leave space for the bulblets that will produce flowers in their own turn. This is how it's done at the Montreal Botanical Gardens. And it will reduce the number of times you have to repot, to every five or six years.

Bulbs purchased in the fall have already undergone a cold treatment before being put on sale. Normally, they will quickly start growing. Depending on the particular cultivar, the flowering period may come as early as a few weeks after planting, and before the appearance of linear leaves, which grow to 24" (60 cm) long.

Should the bulbs take too long to germinate, they can be soaked for two or three hours in 104°F (40°C) water in order to break up the enzymes that control the flowering mechanism. The stalk will then sprout from the tip of the bulb's nose in the days immediately following the procedure.

Keep its neck dry

The amaryllis must be placed under a bright light or in morning sun, at an average temperature of 69-70°F (20-21°C). Keep the soil moist after planting. Water regularly, but only after the first flower buds appear, at the time that the plant starts to take root.

Amaryllis prefer tepid water — or at room temperature. Be careful not to let water fall into the plant's neck. Otherwise, the plant may develop ink-spot fungus, which causes red blotches on the leaves or on the scales of the bulb, often leading to decay. The soil must never be soaking wet; water only when it is slightly dry.

Fertilizing: the secret of success

Once growth is well underway, be sure to fertilize the plant regularly — every two weeks — for about a month. It's an essential secret of success if you want to keep the amaryllis in a healthy condition for a few years. A balanced liquid fertilizer will serve the purpose, as well as a slow release granular type.

On the other hand, at the Montreal Botanical Gardens, they reckon that a 20-20-20 fertilizer makes the growing environment too acidic. Therefore, their amaryllis collection is fertilized alternately with 20-20-20 and 15-5-15. It's entirely possible that you won't be able to find a 15-5-15 solution in stores, but something approaching the same proportions will do the trick.

When the flowering is finished, cut the stalk down to bulb height and carry on fertilizing until the fall even if the plant stays outside during the summer.

In September, with the onset of the first cool nights, bring the amaryllis inside.

A 12-week dry period

The most practical recipe for encouraging the plant to flower again is to put the pot in a cool place, about 60°F (15°C), and stop watering for 12 weeks. Next, transfer the plant to a warmer — say, 70-72°F (20-22°C) — and well-lit location, taking care to remove the dead leaves, leaving any that are undamaged. It will be several weeks until the plant flowers again, often not before the end of winter or beginning of spring.

Then take charge as if it were a new bulb. You can repot just as soon as the first stem grows up from the bulb, changing the soil and always handling the roots with utmost care.

Amaryllis will produce new bulblets each year. You can either leave them where they are or transplant them in a new pot, as long as they have at least one root. However, it will take three or four years before they flower.

Amaryllis belladonna

AMARYLLIS BELLADONNA
Origin: South Africa.
Description: amaryllis family. There is only one species. Fleshy, linear leaves, 10-16" (25-40 cm) long. Stalk: thick, stiff, purple, up to 24" (60 cm) high and topped by an umbel. Flowers: about 6, small and fragrant, trumpet-shaped, 2-4" (6-10 cm) long, 6 petals. Color: pink. Some cultivars have white, dark pink or pink and white flowers.
Cultivation: like other Hippeastrums. Often sold by catalogue.

HIPPEASTRUM PAPILIO
Origin: Brazil.
Description: 5 fluted, linear leaves, 12-20" (30-50 cm) long. Stalk: 10-18" (25-45 cm), at times 24"

(60 cm) in ideal conditions. Flowers: usually 2 per stem, rarely 3. Color: greenish, stained and striped in burgundy red. The "Lima" cultivar is similar in appearance and easier to flower.
Note: especially beautiful, *Hippeastrum papilio* is expensive, because it has a much slower growing period than other cultivars. Unfortunately, it often takes two, even three, years for the plant to flower after you buy it. Consequently, you must be much more patient while you wait for several additional stalks.

Hippeastrum papilio

257

$\mathcal{O}$XALIS
Wood Sorrel

$\mathcal{O}$ xalis in the garden? Well, why on earth not! While they are hugely popular as indoor plants, they can also liven up the flower bed, growing all summer long. As a bonus, you can bring them back into the house at the end of the season and even give some to friends.

They produce small tubers that are easy to keep in vermiculite or peat moss until spring. But be careful! They are occasionally susceptible to decay. Check the tubers frequently during the winter, and get rid of any that aren't in perfect condition.

Oxalis have spread almost everywhere around the globe. There are about 850 species — considered by some people as a mere weed — existing in very diverse habitats, many of them concentrated in South Africa and South America.

Wild species

The plant's name comes from the Greek *oxys*, meaning "acid" or "sour," and refers to the taste of the leaves. It is a member of the *oxalidaceae* family, a group of stemless annuals, perennials and shrubs. Several species have bulbous or tuberous roots. The leaves are clover-like and oxalis is highly prized as a decorative plant. The flowers and leaves are attached to the base by a long, slender peduncle.

Considering the very large number of species — in Canada there are at least three wild species — oxalis are often difficult to classify, sometimes leading to confusion between the scientific nomenclature and the names used commercially.

The dozen or so species sold in the marketplace are commonly advertised under the generic name, oxalis. A number of cultivars are also available.

A thick green carpet

Planted out of doors, oxalis prefer a rich, moist, well-drained soil in a partially shady location. They will flower through most of the summer months and, once established in the flower bed, create a thick green carpet that keeps the weeds at bay.

Multiply by dividing up the clumps or the new rhizomes — also by seed. Oxalis are susceptible to leaf spotting and mildew. Indoor plants are mainly affected by spider mites, mealybugs, kermes and thrips.

Oxalis triangulis *is an indoor plant, but can adorn a flower bed in summertime.*

Internationaal Bloembollen Centrum

OXALIS TRIANGULARIS
Oxalis
Origin: Brazil.
Flowering period: year-long.
Description: delicate, slender peduncle 6-14" (15-35 cm) high, topped by a leaf composed of 3 triangular leaflets, very deep purple, almost black around the edges. The leaves fold up at night. Flowers borne in umbels, from 6-12 and very small. Color: pink.
Cultivation: attractive rock-garden plant. For indoor use, regular well-drained soil, medium light but no direct sun. Occasionally sold as "purple shamrock."

OTHER SPECIES
Oxalis acetosella: native to Asia, Europe and North America. This is a creeping indigenous plant, sold as *O. montana*. Leaves similar to a four-leafed clover. Flower: solitary, ⅓"

(1 cm) across, whitish, veined with purple. Early flowering, slow growing. Overall height: 4" (10 cm).
Oxalis adenophylla: native to the Argentinian and Chilean Andes. Numerous leaves, lightly hairy, shaped like an inverted heart. Flowers: 1" (2.5 cm) across, five petals, tips are dark pink veined with purple, whitish throat but purple at the center. Blooms in late spring. Hardy in Zone 5. Also grown as an indoor plant.
Oxalis regnellii: native to South America, from Peru to Brazil. Very similar to *O. triangularis*.
Oxalis tetraphylla: native to Mexico. Triangular leaves, comprising 4 leaflets, green with purple center and dark pink flowers. Often sold as *Oxalis deppei* (four-leaf clover), that is, when the species name is provided. The "Alba" cultivar has white flowers.

$\mathcal{S}$CADOXUS

Scadoxus

$\mathcal{S}$cadoxus is an indoor plant whose inflorescence resembles an allium. It is a red sphere made up of delicate and graceful star-shaped flowers — sometimes as many as 200. There are a dozen species mainly native to tropical Africa. The name *scadoxus* means "parasol."

There is a good deal of confusion about the name of this plant, especially among marketers.

The species is usually sold under the name *Haemanthus*. Scadoxus is closely related to the amaryllis family, except that it has only two leaves. Experts regard *Haemanthus multiflorus* — the species most often offered by catalogue — as a *Scadoxus*.

Also known as Blood lily, *scadoxus multiflorus* is a bulbous plant with five large fleshy leaves, 12" (30 cm) long and up to 8" (20 cm) wide. The stalk can reach a height of 12" (30 cm), and the diameter of the inflorescence varies from 2¾-4" (7 to 10 cm).

Small orange berries

Plant the bulb so that its neck protrudes from the soil, in an indoor potting mixture, in a sunny location but away from the hot midday sun.

Once it starts to grow, put the pot in a lightly shaded spot. Water frequently and fertilize once a month. When the leaves fade, stop watering. After resting for a few months, the stalk begins growing again. Scadoxus

Jacques Allard

Scadoxus multiflorus

261

normally flowers at the beginning of the summer and is covered later on by a mass of little red berries.

The plant will reproduce by seed or by bulblets picked off when growth gets underway again.

Scadoxus' *inflorescence is formed by a mass of tiny star-shaped flowers.*

$\mathcal{S}$PREKELIA
Orchid Lily

$\mathcal{N}$ative to Guatemala and Mexico, sprekelia is a magnificent indoor bulbous plant, cultivated for its solitary, dark red — often scarlet — flower, resembling a large orchid.

Three long petals joined at the base form a pretty bouquet with long stamens, topped by three more petals, larger and separate, which spread upwards and outwards, creating a lopsided cross.

Flowering takes place in the spring, but sometimes flowers reappear two or even three times in a year if the soil is allowed to dry out for three weeks or a month after they bloom. Unfortunately the flowers last only a short time.

Orchid lily

The plant's scientific name honors Johann Heinrich von Sprekelsen (1691-1764), a German lawyer who was an enthusiastic amateur botanist and gardener. It is also called Orchid lily or Aztec lily, and belongs to the amaryllis family. There is just one species, *S. formosissima*, but a few pale or very dark red variants exist.

Sprekelia has narrow, linear, erect leaves that are pendent at the tips, 16-20" (40 — 50 cm) long. The stalk, 12" (30 cm) long, sometimes grows before the foliage emerges.

Plant the bulb in an indoor potting mixture, being careful to let the neck show above the surface. The plant should be put in a sunny spot. Start watering when growth begins.

Orchid lily

263

A Dormant Period

Fertilize the sprekelia with a balanced plant food every two weeks. Stop watering when the leaves fade. The bulb will then become dormant and can be kept
in a cool place. It's not necessary to repot very often, because a sprekelia likes
to feel snug in its pot.

It can also be planted outside in the garden in a sunny location, but needs
to be kept inside for the winter.

Propagate by transplanting the bulblets picked during dormancy. The plant
is seldom troubled by disease or insects.

$\mathcal{G}$LOSSARY

Alternate leaves: Leaves occurring singly on alternate sides and at different positions along the length of the stem.

Annual: Plant that completes its life cycle in one season, flowering and dying after producing seeds.

Anther: The swollen part of the stamen where pollen is produced.

Axis: Stalk or stem along which other organs (stem, roots, etc.) are arranged and supported.

Axil: Interior of the angle formed by a leaf on a stem.

Basal leaf: A leaf that grows at the base of a plant or from the main stem.

Berry: Soft, fleshy fruit containing seeds.

Biennial: Plant that takes two years to complete its life cycle.

Botrytis: Genus of fungi causing serious plant diseases, attacking the foliage, fruit, bulbs, corms and rhizomes.

Bract: A modified leaf located at the base of a flower or inflorescence. Bracts may be small or large, and are often brightly colored.

Bulb: Underground organ made of overlapping scales that serve as storage reserves.

Bulbil: Small bulb-like organ located on the axil of a leaf which often drops off spontaneously and produces another plant.

Calyx: External envelope of a flower formed by the sepals.

Clone: Individual plant genetically identical to another. Under normal circumstances, bulbils produce clones.

Corm: Short swollen underground stem, sheathed in a papery fibrous tunic, that serves as a storage organ. Crocuses, crocosmia and gladioli are typical corms.

Corolla: The part of a flower formed by the petals.

Corymb: An inflorescence or cluster of flowers that reach the same height although attached to different parts of the stem.

Cultivar: Plant variety raised by artificial horticultural techniques.

Cutting: Piece of a living plant — leaf, stem or root — removed and used for propagating a new plant.

Dentate: Describes a leaf edged with fine, teeth-like notches.

Dormancy: Physiological state of a plant when it rests, in conditions of heat, cold or drought.

Fleshy: Thick, firm; pulpy in fruit

Flower: Reproductive organ of a plant.

Fluted: Describes leaves curled up to form lengthwise grooves.

Forcing: Cultivating a plant outside the normal growing season, often as a means of producing cut flowers or flowering pots.

Fruit: Mature or ripened ovary of a flower containing the seeds that were produced by the fertilization of its male and female parts.

Genus: Homogeneous group of plant species with common characteristics.

Heavy soil: Compact soil, somewhat broken up and permeable, often containing a good portion of clay.

Herbaceous: Describes a plant that goes dormant or dies down at the end of the growing season.

Hybrid: The offspring of parents that belong to different varieties, species or genera.

Incised: Deeply cut.

Indigenous: Applied to plants that grow naturally in their native habitat.

Inflorescence: A cluster of flowers arranged on a single axis.

Lanceolate: Lance-shaped, tapering to a narrow tip.

Leaflet: Part of a compound leaf, resembling a small leaf.

Light soil: Type of soil that can be easily broken up or fragmented.

Linear: Long and uniformly narrow over the entire length.

Mutation: Abrupt modification of genetic characteristics that persist over successive generations.

Naturalized: Said of a plant that grows wild and is then introduced in an area other than its native habitat.

Nematode: Microscopic round worm that can cause extensive damage to leaves and roots, especially in bulbs.

Nomenclature: Systematic naming of plants according to international scientific standards.

Offset: Small bulb (or bulblet) growing from the base of its parent bulb.

Opposite: Describes leaves arranged in pairs along a stem.

Palmate: Describes a leaf arranged like the fingers of a hand, radiating from a center point.

Pedicel: Stalk supporting an individual flower.

Peduncle: Stalk supporting one or more flowers.

Perennial: A hardy plant that can withstand winter conditions and live for a number of years.

Perianth: The sepals and petals of a flower.

Periodism: Control of plant functions by subjecting them to various amounts and times of light and darkness.

Petiole: The stalk of a leaf.

Pistil: The female parts of a flower consisting of the ovary, style and stigma.

Plantlet: Young, small plant at the onset of germination.

Pollen: Powdery, microscopic articles released from the anthers containing the male cells used for fertilization.

Recurved: Describes petals of flowers that curve backward.

Reticulated: Describes a series of lines forming a network or web-like pattern.

Rhizome: Swollen, horizontal underground stem producing roots and shoots.

Rosette: Low flat cluster of leaves arranged like a whorl around the main stem of a plant.

Seed: Fertilized ovule containing an embryo and the reserves necessary to develop as a plant.

Self-propagated: Garden plant that self-seeds and then spreads into its immediate vicinity, and at times even farther away.

Sepal: Part of a calyx, small, green and petal-like.

Sessile: Refers to a leaf, flower, or fruit without a stalk.

Spadix: Fleshy axis of a plant belong to the *Araceae* family (Jack-in-the-pulpit; calla lily), embedded with tiny sessile flowers.

Spathe: Large modified leaf or hood–like bract surrounding a spadix.

Species: Individual plants that share common characteristics and can interbreed freely.

Spider mites: Minuscule creatures endowed with four pairs of legs and resembling spiders. They suck out the sap of plants. There are something like 250,000 species; the most familiar are the _tétranyques_, often called red spider mites.

Spike: Elongated flower cluster, with individual flowers attached perpendicular to the main stem.

Stalk: Long stem or peduncle emanating (starting) from the base of the plant and bearing one or more flowers.

Stamen: Male reproductive organ of a flower that carries the pollen.

Stigma: Part of the pistil forming the upper part of the ovary.

Thrips: Tiny, 1–5mm-long insects that feed on the sap of plants. There are a great many varieties, most of which cause considerable damage.

Tuber: Swollen root or underground stem.

Tuberous: Possessing the characteristics of a tuber.

Umbel: Flower cluster in which individual flowers rise to the same height from the same point on the stem.

Variety: A subdivision of a species. Often used as a synonym for hybrid and cultivar.

Veins: Bundles of fibrous tissue forming a leaf.

ℬIBLIOGRAPHY

A-Z Encyclopedia of Garden Plants. Montreal: Reader's Digest, 1997.

BIRD, Richard. *Lilies*. London: Quintet Publishing, 1991.

Bloembollen Voorjaashloeirs. Lisse: BKD, 1999.

BROTHER MARIE-VICTORIN. *Flore laurentienne*. Montréal: Les presses de l'Université de Montréal, 1995.

Bulbes. Cologne: Könemann, 1999.

DE HERTOGH, August and LE NARD. Marcel, *The Physiology of Flower Bulbs*. Amtersdam: Elesevier, 1993.

DOUCET, Roger. *La science agricole*. Eastman: Éditions Berger, 1994.

Encyclopédie des fleurs et plantes de jardin. Montréal: Sélection du Reader's Digest, 1982.

FORTIN, D. *Plantes vivaces pour le Québec,* vols I, II, III, IV. Saint-Laurent: Trécarré, 1993, 1994, 1995, 1998.

GOODY, Jack. *La culture des fleurs*. Paris: Seuil, 1994.

HESSAYON, D.G. *The House Plant Expert*. London: Expert Books, 1994.

HODGSON, Larry. *Les annuelles*. Boucherville: Broquet, 1999.

HODGSON, Larry. *Les plantes d'intérieur*. Boucherville: Broquet, 1998.

JACOBI, Karlheinz. *Les plus belles fleurs et plantes à bulbes*. Aartselaar: Chantecleer Press, 1996.

KILLINGBACK, Stanley. *Tulips*. London: Quintet Publishing, 1991.

LAMOUREUX, Gisèle. *Plantes sauvages printanières*. Saint-Augustin: Fleurbec, 1992.

LEMMERS, Willeny. *Tulipa, A Photographer's Botanical Artisan*. New York: 1999.

Manuel pour la sélection des cultivars de bulbes à fleurs, part I, 3rd édition. Hillegom: Centre international des bulbes à fleurs, date unknown.

McRAE, Edward A. *Lilies, A Guide for Growers and Collectors*. Portland: Timber Press, 1998.

PHILLIPS, Roger and Martyn RIX. *The Random House Book of Bulbs*. New York: Random House, 1989.

PIRONE, Pascal P. *Diseases and Pests of Ornamental Plants,* 5th ed. New York: Wiley-Interscience Publications, 1978.

PRIEUR, Benoît. *Guide des fleurs pour les jardins du Québec*. Montréal: Les Éditions de l'Homme, 1994.

RAYNAL-ROQUES, Aline. *La botanique redécouverte*. Paris: Belin 1994.

ROSSI, Rossella. *Les plus belles plantes à fleurs*. Portland: Timber Press, 1995.

ROYAL HORTICULTURAL SOCIETY. *Manual of Bulbs*. Portland: Timber Press, 1995.

Sunset National Garden Book. Menlo Park, CA., Sunset Books.

Taylor's Guide to Bulbs. New York: Chantecleer Press, 1986.

VAN SCEEPEN, J. *Classified List and International Register of Tulip Names*. Hillegon: Royal General Bulbgrowers Association, 1996.

VIDALIE, Henri. *Les productions florales*. Paris: Lavoisier, Technique et Documentation, 1990.

VILMORIN, Jean-Baptiste (de) and Marcel CLÉMENT. *Le jardin des hommes*. Crémona: Le pré aux Clers, 1996.

INDEX

"Georgette," 124
"Giuseppe Verdi," 113, 120
"Golden Apeldoorn," 110-111, 113
"Golden Melody," 125
"Gordon Cooper," 113
"Grand Duke," 109
"Green Eyes," 118
"Hamilton," 113, 116
"Johann Strauss," 113
"Juan," 113
"Kees Nelis," 115, 125
"Keizerskroon," 109, 113
"Large Copper," 113
"Madame Lefeber," 113
"Madison Garden," 113
"Maureen," 116
"Menton," 116
"Monssella," 125
"Monte Carlo," 115, 125
"Montréal," 124
"Mount Tacoma," 120
"Orange Bouquet," 124
"Orange Emperor," 113, 120
"Orange Sun," 125
"Oratorio," 120
"Oxford," 113, 115
"Parade," 113
"Peach Blossom," 110, 115
"Pink Emperor," 120
"Pink Impression," 113, 116
"Pinocchio," 113, 120
"Plaisir," 113
"Princess Irene," 113, 125
"Professor Röntgen`," 118
"Purissima," 113
"Québec," 124

"Queen of Night," 110, 116
"Queen of Sheba," 116
"Red Bouquet," 124
"Red Riding Hood," 120
"Red Shine," 116
"Rosario," 113
"Showwinner," 113
"Shakespeare," 113
"Stresa," 113-114, 120
"Sylvia Warder," 124
"Toronto," 11, 113, 124
"Uncle Tom," 120
"Unicum," 121
"Van der Neer," 115
"Van Tubergen," 121
"Viking," 125
"White Emperor," 120
"Zombie," 113

Wake Robin (see *Trillium*), 143
Windflower (see *Anemone*) 150-153, 176
  De Caen variety, 153, 218
  Florists' anemone, 150, 152
  St. Brigid, 153
Winter Aconite (see *Eranthis*), 60-61
Wood Sorrel (see *Oxalis*), 258-260

Zantedeschia (see Calla Lily, Arum Lily), 17, 170, 224-227
  Z. aethiopica, 225
  Z. albomaculata, 225
  Z. elliottiana, 225
  Z. pentlandii, 225
  Z. rehmannii, 225
  "Black Forest," 227
  "Bridal Blush," 226

Printed in Canada